BROKE NO MORE

THE GEN Z GUIDE TO MONEY MASTERY
IN 5 WEEKS

EASY-TO-FOLLOW STRATEGIES TO BUDGET, SAVE, BUILD CREDIT, AND ACHIEVE FINANCIAL FREEDOM

SASHA S. ALBRIGHT

READ THIS FIRST!

Dear Reader,

As a thank you for purchasing "Broke No More" I'd like to gift you my exclusive guide: **"Money Multiplier: Transform Your Savings into a Wealth-Building Machine"** – absolutely FREE!

This powerful companion guide will show you:

- Simple strategies to maximize your savings potential
- Smart investment basics for beginners
- Proven techniques to make your money grow faster
- Expert tips to accelerate your wealth-building journey

Claim Your FREE Guide Now:

Start growing your wealth today!

LOOKING FOR MORE PERSONAL FINANCE RESOURCES?

Visit my website for free tools, guides, and resources to help you continue mastering your finances and achieving your dreams.

💡 **Explore investment tips, budgeting, debt management strategies, and more.**
🔗 **Check it out here: www.Path2Better.com**

This book is for you, Angels. It's a guide to help you navigate the financial world with the same strength and resilience you've shown in overcoming life's challenges. May it empower you to manage your money wisely to pursue your dreams and live the beautiful life you deserve.

With all my love,
Mom

CONTENTS

INTRODUCTION: YOUR FINANCIAL JOURNEY BEGINS HERE

Money. It's the fuel that powers our dreams, the source of our greatest anxieties and most liberating moments. In today's fast-paced world, understanding your finances and managing your money isn't just a useful skill but an essential survival tool. Yet, for many of us, particularly young adults stepping into the world of full-time jobs, rent payments, and student loan debts, the realm of personal finance can feel like a complex maze with no clear exit.

I get it. I've been there too.

I'm not just another finance guru spouting jargon from an ivory tower. I've navigated the treacherous waters of personal finance, made mistakes, learned hard lessons, and come out the other side with a passion for helping others avoid the pitfalls I encountered.

With over two decades of experience in personal finance and investing, my journey began when I was young and first started earning my own money. As an engineer with a degree in economics, I approached personal finance with a curious and analytical mind. I voraciously consumed every finance book I could find, eager to learn from others' mistakes and successes. Despite my best efforts, I still made my fair share of financial missteps along the way. However, these experiences only fueled my passion for mastering money management.

Through diligent saving and smart investing, I achieved a goal many dreams of – retiring from corporate America at the age of 47. This financial freedom has allowed me to pursue my passions, including extensive travel and, most importantly, helping others navigate their financial journeys. I've witnessed firsthand how proper financial education can transform lives, alleviate stress, and open doors to new opportunities.

This transformative power drives me to share my knowledge and experience with you. My goal is to help you avoid the pitfalls I encountered and guide you toward financial success, no matter your starting point.

And that's why I wrote this book.

The world of personal finance can be overwhelming, especially for young adults. You're juggling new responsibilities, trying to establish your career, maybe thinking about buying a car, a home or starting a family. All while dealing with student loans, credit card offers that seem too good to be true (spoiler: they usually are), and the constant pressure to keep up with your peers' lifestyles.

The challenges are real:

- Navigating the job market and negotiating your first salary
- Managing student loan debt that feels insurmountable
- Trying to save for the future when you're barely making ends meet

- Understanding credit scores and how they impact your financial life
- Figuring out how to invest when you can barely afford your daily coffee

These are just a few of the hurdles you might be facing. But here's the good news: you're not alone, and it's not as complicated as it seems.

This book is your roadmap to financial freedom. It's designed to guide you, step by step, through the essentials of money management and personal finance. We'll demystify complex concepts, provide practical strategies you can implement immediately, and help you build a solid financial foundation that will serve you for years.

But this isn't just another dry finance book filled with charts and intimidating equations. What sets "Broke No More" apart is its focus on you—the young professional trying to make sense of your money. We'll explore the psychology behind your money habits, helping you understand why you make your financial decisions. We'll provide real-life examples and scenarios that you can relate to. And most importantly, we'll give you actionable advice to start using today to improve your financial situation.

Here's what you'll discover as we explore the path to financial mastery:

- We'll start by exploring your money mindset, helping you understand and overcome limiting financial beliefs.
- You'll learn how to create a budget that actually works for your lifestyle.
- We'll tackle the beast of debt, giving you strategies to pay it off efficiently.

- You'll discover the secrets of saving, even when you think there's nothing left.
- We'll demystify credit scores and teach you how to use credit cards responsibly.
- We'll discuss how to pay back debt and plan for big financial goals like buying a home.
- Finally, we'll dive into a comprehensive 5-week action plan, providing you with practical, week-by-week steps to manage your money and take control of your finances.

This book is tailored specifically for young professionals like you who are looking to build a solid financial foundation. Whether fresh out of college, a few years into your career, or thinking about making a big life change, you'll find valuable insights and strategies here.

To get the most out of this book, I encourage you to approach it with an open mind and a willingness to change. Read it cover to cover or jump to the sections that are most relevant to your current situation. Take notes, and most importantly, act. Remember, knowledge is power, but only when applied.

As we conclude this introduction, I want you to know that taking control of your finances is one of the most empowering things you can do for yourself. It's not always easy, and there will be challenges along the way. However, with the right knowledge and tools, this book will help you overcome any financial obstacle.

Your financial future starts now. Not tomorrow, not next week, but right here, in this moment. You've already taken the first step towards financial freedom by picking up this book. Now, let's take the next step together.

Are you ready to transform your relationship with money? Go from broke to prosperous? To build the financial future, you've always dreamed of.

Turn the page, and let's begin your journey to financial success. Your future self will thank you for it.

CHAPTER 1
BEHAVIORAL FINANCE AND YOU

UNDERSTANDING YOUR MONEY MINDSET

Your attitudes and beliefs about money are the invisible force shaping your financial destiny. It's the lens through which you view wealth, the voice in your head when you purchase, and the gut feeling you get when you think about your financial future. Understanding and mastering your money mindset is the first crucial step towards financial freedom.

Your money mindset isn't something you're born with; it's a complex construct that begins forming in your earliest years and continues to evolve throughout your life. It's shaped by many factors: your family dynamics, cultural background, personal experiences, and even the media you consume. To truly understand and potentially reshape your money mindset, it's crucial to delve into these formative influences.

Family: The Crucible of Financial Attitudes

Think back on your childhood and adolescence. How did money discussions play out in your household? Were they loaded with tension, marked by hushed whispers, or approached openly and strategically? These early experiences form the foundation of your financial attitudes.

Consider the contrasting experiences of two friends, Sarah and Mike. Sarah grew up in a household where financial literacy was prioritized. Her parents openly discussed budgeting strategies, involved her in financial decisions, and encouraged her to save for her goals. This nurturing financial environment fostered in Sarah a positive money mindset. She views money as a tool for achieving her aspirations rather than a source of anxiety. Today, Sarah navigates her finances with confidence and purpose.

Mike's story paints a different picture. Money was a taboo subject in his family, often leading to intense arguments behind closed doors. This atmosphere of financial secrecy and stress left an indelible mark on Mike's psyche. As a young adult, he found himself grappling with financial anxiety and struggling to implement basic budgeting practices. It wasn't until he recognized the root of his money fears that Mike challenged and reshaped his financial mindset.

Sarah's story illustrates how a nurturing financial environment can foster confidence and purpose. In contrast, Mike's experience shows how financial secrecy can lead to anxiety and struggle. These contrasting tales highlight a crucial point: early money experiences shape adult financial behaviors. However, awareness is the first step towards change. By understanding your financial origin story, you can begin to rewrite it.

Cultural Currents: The Broader Financial Context

Beyond the microcosm of family, your cultural background plays a significant role in molding your money mindset. Different cultures emphasize various aspects of financial management, influencing everything from saving habits to attitudes toward debt and investment strategies.

For instance, many Asian cultures strongly emphasize financial conservatism and long-term planning. There's often a cultural expectation to prioritize saving, avoid debt, and plan for future generations. This mindset can lead to a more cautious approach to financial decisions, focusing on security and stability.

In contrast, some Western cultures, particularly in the United States, often emphasize individualism and present-focused enjoyment. This can translate into a greater willingness to take financial risks, a higher tolerance for debt, and a focus on using money to enhance the current lifestyle rather than solely planning for the future.

Consider the experiences of Maria, who was raised in a Hispanic household, and John, who came from a typical American family. Maria grew up observing her parents regularly send money to extended family, instilling a sense of financial interconnectedness. For her, financial success isn't just about personal wealth; it's about supporting her community. On the other hand, John was encouraged to earn his own money from a young age, fostering a strong sense of financial self-reliance.

Understanding these cultural nuances can provide valuable insights into your own financial behaviors and help you appreciate diverse financial perspectives.

The Media Maze: Navigating Financial Messages

The media plays an increasingly significant role in shaping our money mindsets in our hyper-connected world. From social media influencers displaying lavish lifestyles to news headlines about economic uncertainties, we're constantly bombarded with messages about money, success, and financial well-being.

These messages can be both empowering and harmful. On the one hand, increased access to financial information and resources has the potential to make more accessible financial education and empower people to manage their own finances. On the other hand, the constant bombardment of consumerist messages and inaccurate representations of wealth can foster feelings of inferiority and drive rash financial decisions.

To navigate this media maze, develop a critical eye. Before acting on financial advice from social media or news outlets, ask yourself: Who benefits from this message? Is this consistent with my financial goals and values? By questioning and filtering the financial information you receive, you can maximize the benefits of media exposure while minimizing its potential negative effects on your money mindset.

Unmasking Your Financial Beliefs: Identifying Limiting Thoughts

Now that we've looked into the origins of your money mindset, it's time to shed light on the beliefs that may prevent you from achieving financial success. These "limiting beliefs" are frequently deeply ingrained, operating beneath the surface of our conscious thoughts and influencing our financial behaviors in subtle but significant ways.

Common limiting beliefs include thoughts like:

- "I'll never be good with money."
- "Rich people are greedy or unethical."
- "I don't deserve financial success."
- "Money is the root of all evil."
- "I'll always be in debt."

To identify your own limiting beliefs, try this reflective exercise:

- Take a few moments to think about money. Notice the emotions that arise. Do you feel anxiety, excitement, indifference, or something else?
- Write down your immediate thoughts about money, wealth, and financial success at least once a week. Don't censor yourself; let your thoughts flow freely.
- Look at what you've written at the end of the month. Can you identify any patterns or recurring themes? These might point to your underlying beliefs about money.
- For each belief you've identified, ask yourself: Is this based on fact or assumption? Where did this belief come from? How is it serving me?

This self-reflection process can be uncomfortable, but it's an essential step in reshaping your relationship with money. By regularly examining your thoughts and feelings about finances, you're becoming a detective in your financial story.

The key is to approach this exercise with curiosity rather than judgment. You're not trying to criticize yourself for having these thoughts – you're simply observing them like a scientist collecting data. By the end of the month, you might be surprised at the patterns that emerge.

Reframing Your Financial Narrative: Challenging and Changing Beliefs

Once you've identified your limiting beliefs, the next step is to challenge and reframe them. This isn't about positive thinking or denying reality; it's about examining your beliefs critically and replacing them with more balanced, empowering perspectives.

For example, if you believe "I'll never be good with money," you might challenge this by asking:

- Is this true? Have there been times when I've made good financial decisions?
- What evidence do I have for and against this belief?
- How is this belief affecting my financial behaviors?
- What would change if I believed "I can learn to manage money effectively"?

The goal is to replace limiting beliefs with more empowering alternatives. Here are some examples:

- Instead of "I'll never be good with money," try "I'm learning and improving my financial skills daily."
- Replace "Rich people are greedy" with "Wealth is a tool that can be used for good and bad purposes."
- Instead of "I don't deserve financial success," affirm "I deserve financial well-being, and I'm working towards it."

Remember, changing deep-seated beliefs takes time and consistent effort. Be patient with yourself and celebrate small shifts in your thinking.

Practical Strategies for Mindset Transformation

Transforming your money mindset isn't just about changing your thoughts; it's about taking concrete actions that reinforce your new beliefs and create positive financial habits. Here are some practical strategies to help you on this journey:

Educate Yourself: Knowledge is power, especially when it comes to finances. Commit to continually expanding your financial literacy. Read books, attend workshops, listen to podcasts, or take online courses about personal finance. The more you understand money management, the more confident and empowered you'll feel.

Set Financial Goals: Goals have to be SMART, Specific, Measurable, Achievable, Relevant, and Time-bound. Instead of vague aspirations like "I want to be rich," set concrete goals like "I will save $5,000 for an emergency fund within the next 12 months." This approach makes your financial objectives tangible and trackable.

Practice Mindful Spending: Before making significant purchases, pause and reflect. Ask yourself:

- Does this align with my values and financial goals?
- Is this a want or a need?

This practice can help you make more intentional financial decisions and reduce impulse spending.

Cultivate a Gratitude Practice: Regularly acknowledging what you're grateful for can shift your focus from what you lack to what you have, fostering a sense of abundance. You can even try to keep a gratitude journal where you write down three things you're thankful for each day, including financial blessings, no matter how small.

Visualize Your Financial Success: Take a moment each day to vividly picture your ideal financial future. Imagine waking up without money stress, confidently making financial decisions, and enjoying the freedom of financial stability. This practice can help shift your mindset from scarcity to abundance and motivate you to take positive financial actions.

Surround Yourself with Positive Influences: The people we spend time with can significantly impact our mindset. Seek friends, mentors, or communities with healthy attitudes toward money and can support you in your financial journey.

Celebrate Financial Wins: Acknowledge and celebrate your financial achievements, no matter how small. Paid off a credit card? Treat yourself to a nice (but budget-friendly) dinner. Hit your savings goal for the month? Share the news with a supportive friend. Celebrating progress reinforces positive financial behaviors and boosts your confidence.

Practice Self-Compassion: Financial setbacks are a normal part of the journey. Instead of berating yourself for mistakes, approach them with kindness and curiosity. Ask what you can learn from the experience and how to improve next time.

OVERCOMING EMOTIONAL SPENDING

Emotional spending is the financial equivalent of comfort eating – it feels good at the moment but often leads to regret. In our world of one-click purchases and targeted ads, we're all susceptible to letting our emotions drive our spending. However, understanding your emotional spending triggers is the first step in mastering them. Let's explore how to recognize and overcome these financial impulses.

Understand Your Spending Triggers

To tackle emotional spending, we first need to identify what sets it off. These triggers are the financial equivalent of your ex's Instagram stories – they provoke an immediate, often irrational response.

Stress: The Ultimate Shopping Enabler

Picture this, you've just survived a week of back-to-back exams, your roommate ate your last slice of pizza, and your favorite show ended on a cliffhanger. Suddenly, that new pair of shoes you've been eyeing seems like the perfect pick-me-up. Stress shopping is like trying to put out a fire with gasoline – it might feel good for a second, but it's not solving the real problem.

Peer Pressure: Keeping Up with the Joneses

Remember when your friend group decided matching designer bags were essential for your weekly brunch? That's peer pressure in action. It's the fear of missing out (FOMO) on steroids, convincing you that you need to spend to fit in. But true friends value you for who you are, not what you own.

Boredom: The Silent Wallet Killer

It's a quiet Saturday night, you're alone with your thoughts (scary, I know), and suddenly, you find yourself deep in the Amazon rabbit hole. Boredom shopping is like snacking when you're not hungry – it fills a void temporarily but leaves you feeling unsatisfied and possibly regretful.

Low Self-Esteem: Retail Therapy Gone Wrong

Sometimes, shopping feels like a quick fix for low self-esteem. New clothes, a fresh haircut, or the latest smartphone might temporarily boost your confidence. But using shopping as a band-aid for deeper issues is like trying to fix a leaky roof with duct tape – it's not a long-term solution.

Celebration: When "Treat Yourself" Goes Too Far

You aced that impossible exam, landed your dream internship, or finally mastered the art of doing laundry without turning everything pink. Time to celebrate, right? While it's natural to want to commemorate achievements, going overboard can turn a well-deserved treat into a financial setback.

Social Media: The Highlight Reel Effect

Ah, social media – where everyone's life looks like a perfectly curated magazine spread. It's easy to fall into the comparison trap and feel the need to keep up with the seemingly glamorous lives of influencers and friends. But remember, social media is like a movie trailer – it only shows the best bits.

Recognizing Your Emotional Spending Patterns

Now that we've identified the usual suspects, it's time to play detective with your own spending habits. The key? Keeping a spending journal. Think of it as a diary for your wallet.

For the next month, challenge yourself to track every purchase. Use a notebook, a spreadsheet, or one of those fancy budgeting apps – whatever works for you. After each purchase, jot down:

- What you bought (be specific – "coffee" is different from "triple venti half-sweet non-fat caramel macchiato")
- How much it cost (yes, even that $1 vending machine snack)
- How you were feeling before, during, and after the purchase
- What triggered the purchase (stress, boredom, that Instagram ad stalking you for weeks?)

At the end of the month, review your journal. You might be surprised by the patterns that emerge. Maybe you tend to splurge on takeout after a stressful day at work, or you can't resist a sale email from your favorite store. This self-awareness is like having a financial superpower –the first step to making real changes.

Strategies to Tame the Emotional Spending Beast

Now that you know your spending triggers and patterns, it's time to develop skills to combat emotional spending. Here are some strategies that don't involve living like a hermit or never buying anything fun again. These strategies are all about finding that sweet spot between responsible spending and still enjoying life

1. Set Concrete Financial Goals

Having clear financial goals is like having a GPS for your money. Whether paying off your student loans, saving for a down payment on a house, or building an emergency fund, having a specific target gives you a reason to think twice before making an impulse purchase.

Make your goals SMART: Specific, Measurable, Achievable, Relevant, and Time-bound. Instead of "save money," try "save $3,000 for a Europe trip in 18 months." Write these goals down and keep them somewhere visible – your phone wallpaper, a sticky note on your mirror, or tattooed on your forehead (okay, maybe not that last one).

2. Find Alternative Stress Relief: Beyond Retail Therapy

Instead of hitting "add to cart" when stressed, find healthier ways to unwind. Exercise is a great option – it's free, releases endorphins, and doesn't clutter up your closet. Try a yoga video on YouTube, go for a run, or have a dance party in your living room.

Stressed? Try a 10-minute meditation or a brisk walk. Bored? Learn a new skill through free online courses. Seeking a mood boost? Call a friend or volunteer for a cause you care about. Create a list of go-to activities for different emotions, so you're prepared when the urge to shop strikes.

3. The "Needs vs. Wants" Showdown

Before purchasing, channel your inner game show host and play "Needs vs. Wants." A need is essential for survival or basic functioning – food, shelter, and clothing. A want is everything else.

This doesn't mean you can never buy wants, but it helps you prioritize. That new video game? Definitely a want. Groceries? Need. New shoes because your only pair has more holes than Swiss cheese? Probably a need. Limited edition, glow-in-the-dark sneakers? You guessed it – want.

4. Practice Mindful Spending: The 24-Hour Rule

Implement a personal waiting period before making non-essential purchases. See something you "must have"? Ask yourself: Do I need this? Will I still want it tomorrow? How will I feel about this purchase in a month? This simple mindfulness practice can help break the automatic cycle of emotional spending.

Wait 24 hours before buying it. Often, the urge passes, and you realize you didn't need it after all.

For bigger purchases, extend this waiting period. A good rule of thumb: For every $100 the item costs, wait one day. That $500 smartwatch? Give it a five-day cooldown period.

5. Budget for Fun: Because Life Shouldn't Be All Ramen and Spreadsheets

Creating a budget doesn't mean sucking all the joy out of life. In fact, budgeting for fun is crucial for long-term financial health. It's like including cheat meals in a diet – it makes the whole plan more sustainable.

Allocate a specific monthly amount for "fun money" or "no questions asked" spending. This allows you to indulge occasionally without derailing your entire financial plan. Whether it's concert tickets, a new book, or that artisanal coffee you love, knowing you have guilt-free spending money can actually reduce the urge to overspend.

Now, I know what you're thinking: "Budget? Isn't that just a fancy word for 'financial straitjacket'?" But hold onto your piggy banks because we'll flip that notion on its head in Chapter 3. That's right, we've got a whole chapter dedicated to the art of budgeting coming up, and trust me, it's not as scary as it sounds.

Practical Tips for Managing Emotional Spending

Now that we've covered the big strategies, let's dive into some practical, everyday tips to keep emotional spending in check:

Unsubscribe from Store Emails: Those "50% OFF EVERYTHING!" emails are designed to trigger impulse buys. Unsubscribe or use a separate email address to shop to reduce temptation.

Use Cash for Discretionary Spending: There's something about handing over physical cash that makes spending feel more real. Try withdrawing your "fun money" in cash at the start of each month.

Find a Financial Accountability Buddy: Share your goals with a friend and check in regularly. It's like having a gym buddy but for your wallet.

Practice Gratitude: Regularly reflect on what you're thankful for. It shifts your focus from what you lack to what you have, reducing the urge to buy more stuff.

Create a "Wish List": When you feel the urge to buy something, add it to a wish list instead. Revisit the list in a month – you'll often find the urge has passed.

Avoid Tempting Environments: If you know browsing the mall leads to overspending, find alternative activities. Meet friends for a picnic in the park instead of at the shopping center.

Use Apps to Your Advantage: Many budgeting apps can send alerts when you're nearing your spending limit in certain categories.

Balancing Enjoyment and Financial Responsibility

Finding the sweet spot between enjoying life and being financially responsible is an art – it takes practice and a bit of finesse.

Prioritize Your Spending: Identify what truly brings you joy and allocate your resources accordingly. Maybe you love trying new restaurants but don't care much about the latest fashion. Spend on experiences that matter to you and cut back on areas that don't.

Create a "Fun Fund": Set aside a specific monthly amount for spontaneous purchases or experiences. It's like giving yourself an allowance – when it's gone, it's gone, but you can spend it guilt-free.

Plan for Big Expenses: Want to go to a music festival next summer? Start saving now. Breaking big expenses into smaller, monthly savings goals makes them more achievable and less likely to derail your finances.

Enjoy Free or Low-Cost Activities: Get creative with how you have fun. Host a potluck dinner party instead of eating out, explore free days at museums, or discover the hiking trails in your area.

The Social Media Spending Trap

In the age of Instagram influencers and TikTok trends, social media can be a minefield for emotional spending. Here's how to navigate it:

Curate Your Feed: Unfollow accounts that make you feel inadequate or trigger spending urges. Instead, follow accounts that inspire you to be financially responsible or content with what you have.

Remember the Highlight Reel Effect: People highlight their best moments on social media, not their financial struggles or buyer's remorse. Don't compare your behind-the-scenes to someone else's highlight reel.

Be Critical of Influencer Recommendations: Remember, many influencers are paid to promote products. Ask yourself if you need that miracle face cream or are just caught up in the hype.

Practice Digital Detox: Occasionally take breaks from social media. Use that time to focus on your goals, enjoy the present moment, or connect with friends in person.

Your Financial Emotions, Your Control

Mastering your emotional spending isn't about depriving yourself or never indulging. It's about understanding your triggers, making conscious choices, and aligning your spending with your values and long-term goals. It's a journey, not a destination, and it's okay to have setbacks along the way.

Remember, every purchase is a choice – a vote for the kind of life you want to live. By becoming aware of your emotional spending triggers and implementing strategies to manage them, you're taking control of your financial future. You're saying yes to financial freedom, peace of mind, and the ability to spend on what truly matters to you.

So, the next time you feel the urge to buy something on impulse, pause and ask yourself: Is this aligned with my goals? Is there a better way to address what I'm feeling right now? Your future self (and bank account) will thank you for it.

Your money mindset is the foundation upon which your financial future is built. By understanding its origins, challenging limiting beliefs, and consistently practicing positive financial habits, you're not just improving your relationship with money – you're opening up a world of possibilities for your financial future.

As you move forward, carry this empowering truth with you: *You have the power to shape your money mindset and, in doing so, to shape your financial destiny*. The journey of a thousand miles begins with a single step – and you've already taken that step by engaging with this book. Keep moving forward, stay curious, and watch as your evolving money mindset transforms your finances and entire perspective on life's opportunities and potential.

COGNITIVE BIASES AND FINANCIAL DECISIONS

We'd all like to think we're rational beings, especially regarding money. But the truth is, our brains are wired with cognitive biases – mental shortcuts that can lead us astray in our financial decisions. Understanding these biases is like having a financial superpower. It lets you recognize when your brain might be tricking you, helping you make more informed choices. Let's unmask these cognitive tricksters and learn how to outsmart them.

What Are Cognitive Biases, Anyway?

Think of cognitive biases as your brain's GPS taking shortcuts. Sometimes, these shortcuts work great, getting you to your destination quickly. Other times, they lead you into a metaphorical ditch. In the world of finance, these mental shortcuts can be the difference between growing your wealth and making costly mistakes.

Some of the most common cognitive biases that love to crash your financial party include:

Confirmation Bias: The "I Knew It All Along" Syndrome

Imagine you're convinced that investing in a startup making flavored dental floss is the next big thing. Every article about dental hygiene suddenly seems like a sign confirming your genius. Meanwhile, you're conveniently ignoring all data suggesting most people prefer plain mint. Confirmation bias is your brain's tendency to seek information supporting your beliefs while ignoring contradictory evidence.

Overconfidence Bias: The "I'm Basically a Financial Genius" Delusion

This voice in your head whispers, 'You've got this!' right before you make a spectacularly bad decision. In the financial world, it might lead you to believe you can time the market perfectly or that your investment choices are foolproof. Spoiler alert: even the pros can't do this consistently.

Sunk Cost Fallacy: The "I've Come This Far, Might as Well Keep Going" Trap

This is the financial equivalent of sitting through a terrible movie just because you've already watched the first hour. It's the reluctance to abandon a plan or investment when it's clearly not working, simply because you've already put time, money, or effort into it. You continue to pour money into a failing side business because you've already invested so much, even though all signs point to it being a lost cause.

How These Biases Mess With Your Money

Now that we've met these troublemakers, let's see how they can turn your financial life into their personal playground:

1. Confirmation Bias: The Echo Chamber Effect

This bias can significantly influence your financial decisions. It often leads to a situation where you surround yourself with information that only confirms your existing beliefs. This creates what's known as an "echo chamber" effect, where your own ideas and opinions are amplified and reinforced while contradictory information is filtered out or ignored.

This self-reinforcing cycle can be particularly dangerous in financial decision-making. It may cause you to overlook important, potentially contradictory information crucial for making well-informed choices.

For instance, let's say you're convinced that real estate is the only way to invest. You might obsessively read articles about successful property investors, join real estate forums, and talk only to friends who've made money on property. Meanwhile, you're missing other potentially lucrative investment opportunities because you're not even considering them.

To break free from this bias, force yourself to play devil's advocate. When you're sure about a financial decision, actively seek opposing viewpoints. It's like trying on different pairs of glasses – you might be surprised at how differently things look from another perspective.

2. Overconfidence Bias: The Financial Icarus

Remember Icarus from Greek mythology? The guy who flew too close to the sun because he thought his wax wings were invincible. That's overconfidence bias in a nutshell. This can lead to taking on way more risk than you can handle in the financial world.

You might think you're immune to market trends, capable of picking winning stocks every time, or able to time the market perfectly. Spoiler alert: even the pros can't do this consistently.

This bias often shows up when people start investing. After a few successful trades, they might think they've cracked the code and start making bigger, riskier bets. It's like thinking you're ready for the Poker World Series because you won a few games with your friends.

To keep this bias in check, always assume you know less than you think you do. Stay humble, keep learning, and don't be afraid to admit when you're unsure. It's okay to say, "I don't know" – it's actually a sign of financial maturity.

3. Sunk Cost Fallacy: The "But I've Already Spent So Much" Spiral

We have already talked about this one. This is the bias that keeps you throwing good money after bad. It's like continuing to water a dead plant, hoping it'll somehow spring back to life.

In the financial world, this might look like:

- Continuing to invest in a losing stock because you've already invested so much money.
- Refusing to drop out of an expensive degree program that you hate and has poor job prospects just because you've already completed two years.
- Keeping a money-draining car because you've already spent so much on repairs.

The key to overcoming this bias is to focus on the future, not the past. Ask yourself: "Regardless of what I've already spent, what's the best decision for my future?" It's like deciding whether to finish a meal when you're already full – just because you paid for it doesn't mean you have to make yourself sick eating it all.

How to Outsmart Your Biased Brain

Now that we've unmasked these cognitive tricksters, let's talk about how to show them who the boss is. Here are some strategies to keep your financial decisions more rational than a Vulcan accountant:

The "Prove Yourself Wrong" Challenge:

Before making a financial decision, seek information that contradicts your belief. If you think a particular investment is a sure thing, research potential downsides or risks.

The "What Would Warren Do?" Method:

When facing a financial decision, ask yourself what an expert you admire would do in your situation. This can help you step outside your biases and look at the situation objectively. Just don't actually call Warren Buffett – he's probably busy.

The "Future You" Visualization:

Before a financial decision, visualize how your future self will be affected. Imagine yourself five or ten years down the line – how will this decision impact that version of you?

The "Phone a Friend" Lifeline:

Sometimes, we're too close to our situation to see it. Talking through your financial decisions with a trusted friend or family can provide a valuable outside perspective. Just make sure it's someone who'll give you honest feedback, not just tell you what you want to hear.

The "Sleep On It" Rule:

For big financial decisions, implement a mandatory waiting period. Sleep on it, or give it a few days or weeks if possible. This cooling-off period can help you move past the initial emotional response and make a more rational decision.

The "Pre-Mortem" Analysis:

Before a significant financial move, imagine it has failed spectacularly. Work backwards to figure out what could have gone wrong. This exercise can help you identify potential pitfalls you might have overlooked.

The "Diverse Input" Strategy:

Actively seek out diverse perspectives on financial matters. Follow financial experts with different viewpoints, read various financial publications, and discuss with people from different financial backgrounds.

Putting It All Together: Your Bias-Busting Toolkit

Now that we've explored these strategies, let's put together a practical toolkit you can use to keep cognitive biases at bay:

The Bias Check Checklist:

Before making any significant financial decision, run through this quick checklist:

Have I considered opposing viewpoints?

- Am I being overconfident in my abilities or knowledge?

- Am I making this decision because of what I've already invested?
- How would I advise a friend in this situation?
- How does this align with my long-term financial goals?

Set aside time each month for a "bias audit." Review your recent financial decisions and ask yourself:

Were there any decisions I made too quickly or without enough information?

- Did I ignore any red flags or warning signs?
- Was I influenced by recent events or media hype?
- Did I seek diverse opinions or stick to sources confirming my beliefs?

This regular check-in can help you stay aware of your biases and improve your decision-making over time.

Find a friend who's also interested in improving their financial decision-making. Agree to be each other's "Bias Buddies." Before making major financial decisions, discuss them with your Bias Buddy. They can help spot biases you might be blind to, and you can do the same for them.

Commit to ongoing financial education. This doesn't mean you need to get an economics degree – even setting aside 15 minutes daily to read about personal finance can make a big difference. The more you understand finance, the better you'll be able to recognize and counter biases.

Embracing Your Biased, Beautiful Brain

Remember, we'll never be completely free of cognitive biases. They're hardwired into our brains. The goal isn't to eliminate them but to recognize when they're influencing us and have strategies to counteract their effects. By understanding these biases and implementing these strategies, you're not just managing your money but mastering your mind. Every financial decision becomes an opportunity to outsmart your biases and make choices aligned with your true financial goals.

With this newfound awareness, we're better equipped to tackle one of the most fundamental aspects of financial health: saving. In the next chapter, we'll dive into "The Art of Saving," where we'll apply our knowledge of behavioral finance to develop strategies that work with our natural tendencies rather than against them. Let's turn our financial self-awareness into actionable saving strategies to build the foundation for your financial future.

YOUR OPINION MATTERS!

Dear Reader,

As you've reached this point in "Broke no More: The Gen Z Guide to Money Mastery in 5 Weeks," I hope you've gained valuable insights and practical strategies to transform your financial life.

Why Your Review is Important

Your feedback is invaluable. It helps:

- Other young adults decide if this book is right for their financial journey
- I understand how to improve and create even better resources for Gen Z's financial education
- Boost the visibility of this book, allowing it to reach more people who could benefit from these money mastery strategies.

Ready to Share Your Thoughts? It takes just a few minutes to make a big impact. Leave Your Review Here

Looking for More Personal Finance Resources?

Visit my website for free tools, guides, and resources that will help you continue mastering your finances and achieving your dreams.

💡 **Explore investment tips, budgeting, debt management strategies, and more.**
🔗 **Check it out here: www.Path2Better.com**

CHAPTER 2
THE ART OF SAVING

WHY SAVING IS ESSENTIAL

Imagine your financial life as a road trip. Your destination is far off, and the journey is unpredictable. In this scenario, having a full tank of gas and some extra cash for unexpected detours isn't just smart—it's essential. That's exactly what saving money is like in the journey of life. Your fuel, backup plan, and ticket to freedom are all rolled into one.

Welcome to the saving world, where we transform your hard-earned money into a powerful financial security and personal growth tool. Whether you're just starting your career or looking to improve your financial habits, understanding the importance of saving is crucial for your financial well-being.

Life has a way of throwing curveballs when we least expect them. Having savings is like having a financial safety net that catches you when these unexpected events occur. It's not about being pessimistic; it's about being prepared.

Imagine you're six months into a new job, feeling financially stable, when suddenly your car breaks down. Without savings, this crisis could force you into high-interest debt. But with a robust savings habit, you can handle this setback without breaking a sweat. You'll be able to get your car repaired and continue with your life, all without the added stress of figuring out how to pay for it.

The Emergency Fund: Your Financial First Aid Kit

An emergency fund is your financial safety net, designed to catch you when life throws its inevitable curveballs. Think of it as your financial first aid kit—you hope you won't need it, but you're incredibly glad it's there when you do.

Financial experts often recommend saving enough to cover three to six months of living expenses. This might sound daunting, especially if you're just starting. The key is to start small and build consistently. Even setting aside $50 a month can make a difference. When that unexpected car repair or medical bill comes along, you'll be prepared to handle it without derailing your entire financial plan.

Let's say you're a freelancer or working in the gig economy. Your income might be variable, making an emergency fund even more crucial. Start by saving just $50 a month. Over time, as your income grows, you can increase this amount. Then, when a major client delays payment or work slows down, you'll have a cushion to fall back on, turning a potentially stressful situation into a manageable one.

Saving for Major Purchases: Avoiding the Debt Trap

Another significant advantage of saving is making major purchases without going into debt. Whether buying a car, putting a down payment on a house, or investing in further education, having savings means achieving these goals without the burden of high-interest payments.

Picture yourself dreaming of a European vacation. Instead of charging it to your credit card and paying it off (with interest) for months or years, you save for it. You create a dedicated travel savings account and set aside a portion of your income each month. It might take longer to reach your goal, but when you finally embark on your adventure, you'll enjoy it much more, knowing it's fully paid for and won't follow you home in debt.

The Power of Compound Interest: Your Money Working for You

Compound interest is like a snowball rolling down a hill, growing larger as it collects more snow. In financial terms, it's the interest you earn not just on your original savings but on the interest you've already earned.

Let's break this down with a simple example. Say you start saving $200 a month at age 25 in an account that earns 5% interest annually. By age 65, you'll have contributed $96,000 of your own money. But thanks to compound interest, your account could actually be worth over $300,000. That's an extra $200,000 just for being patient and consistent.

This example illustrates why starting to save early is so powerful. The longer your money has to grow, the more dramatic the effects of compound interest. However, it's never too late to start. Even if you're starting later in life, compound interest can still work magic—you might need to save a bit more to reach your goals.

Saving for Major Purchases: Avoiding the Debt Trap

Another significant advantage of saving is making major purchases without going into debt. Whether buying a car, putting a down payment on a house, or investing in further education, having savings means achieving these goals without the burden of high-interest payments.

Picture yourself dreaming of a European vacation. Instead of charging it to your credit card and paying it off (with interest) for months or years, you save for it. You create a dedicated travel savings account and set aside a portion of your income each month. It might take longer to reach your goal, but when you finally embark on your adventure, you'll enjoy it much more, knowing it's fully paid for and won't follow you home in debt.

Paying Yourself First: Prioritizing Your Financial Future

The concept of "paying yourself first" is a powerful strategy in personal finance. It means prioritizing your savings before spending on discretionary items. When you receive your income, you first allocate a portion to your savings, treating it like a non-negotiable expense.

Imagine you've just started a new job with a slightly higher salary. Instead of letting that extra money disappear into increased spending, you save it. You set up an automatic transfer that moves 15% of each paycheck into a savings account before you even have a chance to spend it. At first, you might feel the pinch, but soon, you adjust your lifestyle to your remaining income. Months later, you'll be amazed at how much you've accumulated without feeling deprived.

Setting and Achieving Financial Goals

Saving is essential for achieving both short-term and long-term financial goals. Short-term goals might include creating an emergency fund, saving for a vacation, or purchasing a new appliance. Long-term goals could be buying a house, starting a business, or planning retirement.

Let's say you have a vision of starting your own business. You know you'll need capital to get started. By setting a clear savings goal and creating a plan to achieve it, you can accumulate the necessary funds without relying on loans or investors. You might cut unnecessary expenses, take on a side gig, or find creative ways to increase your income. Each step brings you closer to your goal, and the discipline you develop in saving will serve you well as a future business owner. In the next section, we will learn how to set financial goals more thoroughly.

The Value of Saving: Peace of Mind and Freedom

Saving money isn't just about having a bigger bank balance—it's about creating peace of mind and freedom in your life. It reduces the stress of living paycheck to paycheck and worrying about unexpected expenses. It gives you the power to make choices based on what's best for you, not just what you can afford at the moment.

Remember, saving doesn't mean depriving yourself of the present. It's about striking a balance that allows you to enjoy life now while securing your future. Even small, consistent savings can accumulate to significant amounts over time. Be patient with yourself, celebrate your progress, and stay committed to your saving goals. Your future self will thank you for the financial foundation you're building today.

TIPS FOR EFFECTIVE SAVING STRATEGIES

Now that you understand why saving is essential, let's dive into how you can become a saving champion. Think of these strategies as your financial toolkit – each a powerful instrument to help you build your savings fortress. Whether you're just starting your saving journey or looking to supercharge your existing habits, these tips will help you save more effectively and efficiently.

Imagine trying to hit a target while blindfolded. Pretty challenging, right? That's what saving without clear goals is like. Setting specific financial goals gives the purpose and direction of your saving effort.

When you set clear financial goals, you create a roadmap for your financial future. Instead of vaguely thinking, "I should save more," you're giving yourself concrete targets to aim for. This specificity makes your saving efforts more focused and meaningful.

Let's say you dream of taking a year off to travel the world. That's a great aspiration, but it's not yet a goal. Turn it into a goal by getting specific: "I want to save $20,000 in the next two years for a year-long world trip." Now, you have a clear target and a timeline, making it much easier to plan your saving strategy.

How to Set Your Financial Goals

- Be Specific: Define exactly what you're saving for. Instead of "save for the future," try "save $5,000 for a down payment on a car."
- Make It Measurable: Attach a specific dollar amount to

your goal. This lets you track your progress and know when you've achieved it.

- Ensure It's Achievable: While it's good to challenge yourself, make sure your goal is realistic given your current financial situation.
- Keep It Relevant: Your goal should align with your values and long-term financial objectives. If owning a home isn't your priority, don't set it as a goal because others are doing it.
- Set a Time Frame: Having a deadline creates a sense of urgency and helps you stay focused.

Automating Your Savings

Once you've set your goals, it's time to make saving effortless. This is where automation comes in. Think of it as putting your savings on autopilot – once you set it up, it happens without you having to think about it.

Automating your savings takes willpower out of the equation. You don't have to remember to transfer money to your savings account or resist the temptation to spend it. It happens automatically, ensuring that you're consistently saving towards your goals.

Most banks allow you to set up recurring transfers from your checking account to your savings account. Choose an amount that fits your budget and schedule the transfers to coincide with your payday.

Savings apps have revolutionized how we approach saving money, making the process more engaging and fun. Let's explore four popular apps that can help gamify your savings journey:

- **Qapital:** This app offers highly customizable saving rules, allowing you to round up purchases or use the "Payday Divvy" feature to distribute your paycheck into different saving goals. Its unique charm lies in quirky rule options, like saving money when your favorite sports team wins. With FDIC-insured savings accounts and shared goal capabilities, Qapital provides a flexible and secure saving experience that can adapt to your specific preferences and lifestyle.
- **Acorns:** Combining saving with investing, Acorns rounds up your purchases to the nearest dollar and invests the difference in a diversified ETF portfolio. It's an excellent choice for those looking to grow their financial knowledge, offering educational content about investing alongside your savings. The standout "Found Money" program allows you to earn additional investments by shopping with partner retailers, maximizing your savings and investing potential with everyday purchases.
- **Digit:** Perfect for those preferring a hands-off approach, Digit analyzes your income and spending patterns to automatically move small, affordable amounts into a separate savings account. This clever app adapts to your spending habits, ensuring you save without feeling the pinch. Its "no overdraft guarantee" provides peace of mind, promising to reimburse any overdraft fees caused by its automatic savings feature, making it a trustworthy companion in your saving journey.
- **Long Game Savings:** Transforming saving into an exciting game, Long Game Savings offers FDIC-insured accounts and the chance to win cash prizes through games when you save. Using prize-linked savings motivates users like a lottery but without the risk of losing money. This approach makes saving thrilling,

offering instant gratification through games and potential prizes, perfect for those who thrive on competition and rewards in their financial journey.

Each of these apps takes a different approach to gamifying savings. Qapital offers the most customization, Acorns combines saving with investing, Digit automatically saves you, and Long Game Savings turns saving into a game with real cash prizes. Choose the one that aligns best with your saving style and what motivates you most.

Remember, while these apps can make saving more fun and easier, they're tools to help you save, not magical solutions. You'll still need to commit to your savings goals and manage your overall budget effectively.

Reducing Unnecessary Expenses

Now that you're automatically saving, let's look at ways to increase the amount you can save. One of the most effective methods is to reduce unnecessary expenses. This doesn't mean living like a monk – it's about being mindful of where your money is going and cutting out expenses that don't add value to your life.

Every dollar you're not spending is a dollar you could be saving. Identifying and eliminating unnecessary expenses frees up more money toward your savings goals. Plus, this process helps you become more aware of your spending habits, which is crucial for long-term financial health. Here are some tips to help you identify and eliminate unnecessary expenses.

- **Track Your Spending:** Before you can cut expenses, you need to know where your money is going. Use a budgeting app or a simple spreadsheet to track all your expenses for a month. You might be surprised at what you discover.

- **Identify Non-Essential Spending:** Look through your expenses and identify items that aren't essential. This could be subscriptions you rarely use, frequent dining out, or impulse purchases.
- **Implement the 30-day Rule:** For non-essential purchases, especially big ones, wait 30 days before buying. This cooling-off period often helps you realize whether you really need the item or if it was just a momentary desire.
- **Find Free or Low-Cost Alternatives:** Look for free or cheaper alternatives to your regular expenses. This could mean switching from gym membership to home workouts or replacing cable TV with a cheaper streaming service.
- **Negotiate Bills:** Many bills, such as insurance premiums or internet services, can be negotiated. Call your providers and see if you can get a better rate.

For example, after tracking your expenses, you might realize you're spending $100 monthly on rarely used subscriptions. Cancelling these could free up $1,200 a year towards your savings goals.

Embracing Lifestyle Changes for Savings Success

As we've explored the importance of saving and various strategies to boost your savings, it's time to consider how small adjustments in your daily life can significantly impact your financial goals. Remember, these changes don't need to be drastic – the consistent, small efforts often yield the most substantial results over time.

Let's dive into some practical ways you can adjust your lifestyle to support your saving goals:

Master the Art of Home Cooking: One of the most effective ways to save money is by planning meals and cooking at home. Not only is this often healthier, but it can also be a fun way to explore new recipes and skills. For instance, by preparing your meals at home and bringing lunch to work, you could save $50-$100 per week. Over a year, that's a potential $2,600-$5,200 in savings – a substantial contribution to your financial goals!

Optimize Your Energy Use: Your utility bills offer another opportunity for savings. Simple changes like switching to LED bulbs, adjusting your thermostat by a few degrees, and unplugging devices when not in use can lead to noticeable reductions in your monthly expenses. These adjustments benefit your wallet and contribute to a more sustainable lifestyle.

Rethink Your Transportation: If your situation allows, consider alternatives to driving everywhere. Public transportation, carpooling, or biking for your commute can save on gas, parking, and vehicle maintenance costs. Plus, you might find these options less stressful and more environmentally friendly.

Shop with Intention: Before making a purchase, especially a significant one, pause and ask yourself: "Is this a need or a want?" Giving yourself time to reflect can often prevent impulse buys and keep you aligned with your saving goals. This mindful approach to shopping can lead to substantial savings over time.

Embrace DIY and Skill-Sharing: In our connected world, you can find online tutorials for almost any simple repair or maintenance task. Learning these skills not only saves money but can also be incredibly satisfying. Furthermore, consider skill-sharing with friends – perhaps you can offer to cut their hair in exchange for help with car maintenance. This approach not only saves money but also strengthens your social connections.

By implementing these lifestyle adjustments, you're saving money and cultivating habits that align with your broader financial goals. As we'll explore in later chapters, these small changes compound over time, creating a solid foundation for your financial future.

Overcoming Psychological Barriers to Saving

As explored in Chapter 1, our money mindset plays a crucial role in our financial behaviors. When it comes to saving, several psychological barriers can hinder our progress. Understanding and addressing these barriers is key to developing a sustainable saving habit.

One significant obstacle is the instant gratification bias. Our brains are wired to prefer immediate rewards over future benefits, making it challenging to save for long-term goals. To overcome this, try visualizing your future self-enjoying the benefits of your savings. Additionally, set small, achievable saving milestones to create a sense of immediate progress and satisfaction.

Another common barrier is loss aversion. We tend to feel the pain of losing money more acutely than the pleasure of gaining it. This can make saving feel like a sacrifice rather than an opportunity. To counter this, reframe saving as 'paying your future self' rather than 'losing' current spending power. View it as an investment in your future freedom and opportunities.

For those who have struggled financially in the past, a scarcity mindset can make saving seem impossible. If you find yourself in this situation, start with very small, regular savings to prove it's possible. Celebrate every saving milestone, no matter how small. These small victories can help shift your mindset from scarcity to possibility.

By recognizing and addressing these psychological barriers, you can create a saving habit that feels empowering rather than restrictive. Remember, changing your saving behavior isn't just about willpower – it's about understanding and reshaping your relationship with money.

Making Saving Fun

Saving doesn't have to feel like a chore. By making it enjoyable, you'll stick with it long-term. Here are some ways to inject some fun into your saving efforts:

- **Savings Challenges:** Participate in savings challenges like the 52-week challenge, where you save an increasing amount each week. Start with $1 in week one, $2 in week two, and so on. By the end of the year, you'll have saved $1,378!
- **Gamify Your Savings:** Use apps that turn saving into a game with rewards and achievements. Some apps even let you compete with friends, adding a social element to saving.
- **Reward Milestones:** Set up a reward system for when you hit certain savings milestones. This could be as simple as attending a movie night when you reach 25% of your goal.
- **Visualize Your Progress:** Create a visual representation of your savings progress, like a thermometer you can color in as you get closer to your goal. Seeing your progress can be very motivating.

While it's great to have big, long-term savings goals, setting smaller, more immediately achievable goals is also important. These "quick wins" can boost your motivation and help build momentum.

Small goals are less overwhelming and provide more frequent positive reinforcement. Each time you achieve a small goal, you build confidence in your ability to save, which can help you tackle larger goals. Here is some advice on how to set small goals.

- **Break Down Larger Goals:** Take your big savings goal and break it into smaller, monthly, or weekly targets.
- **Make it a Game:** Challenge yourself to save a certain amount quickly, like $100 weekly.
- **Focus on Percentages:** Instead of fixed amounts, save a certain percentage of your monthly income, gradually increasing it over time.

For instance, if you aim to save $1,200 for a new laptop in a year, break it down to saving $100 monthly. This feels much more manageable and allows you to celebrate small victories along the way.

Tracking Expenses to Identify Unnecessary Spending

You can't manage what you don't measure. Tracking your expenses is crucial for understanding your spending habits and identifying areas where you can cut back.

Expense tracking gives you a clear picture of where your money is going. Often, we underestimate how much we're spending in specific categories. By tracking, you might discover that your daily coffee habit costs you $100 a month or that you're spending more on subscriptions than you realized. Here you have a few methods you can use to track your expenses:

- **Keep Receipts:** Keeping receipts is invaluable for cash purchases or when you want more detailed information. If you struggle with holding onto paper receipts, consider taking a photo with your smartphone as soon as you receive them. This digital method ensures you have a record of every purchase, even if you misplace the physical receipt. Regularly reviewing these receipts can help you catch any discrepancies in your spending and provide a more accurate picture of your cash expenses.
- **Use Budgeting Apps:** In today's digital age, budgeting apps have become powerful tools for expense tracking. Apps like Mint, YNAB (You Need A Budget), or Personal Capital can automatically import and categorize your transactions from linked bank accounts and credit cards. These apps provide visual representations of your spending patterns, making it easy to identify areas where you might be overspending. Many also offer bill reminders and goal-tracking features, helping you stay on top of your overall financial picture.
- **Review Bank and Credit Card Statements:** Make it a habit to go through your bank and credit card statements each month. This practice not only helps you track your expenses but also allows you to catch any fraudulent charges or errors. As you review, categorize each expense. This process can reveal spending patterns you might not have noticed otherwise, such as how much you're really spending on dining out or subscription services.

- **Create a Simple Spreadsheet:** For those who prefer a hands-on approach, creating a spreadsheet can effectively track expenses. This method gives you complete control over categorizing and analyzing your spending. You can customize your spreadsheet to fit your specific needs. While it requires more manual input than automated apps, a spreadsheet can provide a deeper understanding of your finances as you actively engage with each entry.

After tracking your expenses for a month, you might find that you're spending $200 on entertainment. If you decide this is more than you'd like, you could set a goal to reduce this to $100 next month, instantly freeing up $100 for your savings.

Remember, becoming a successful saver is a journey, not a destination. It's about building habits and making choices that align with your financial goals. Start by setting clear, achievable goals. Then, make saving automatic so you don't rely on willpower alone. Look for ways to reduce unnecessary expenses and make your money work harder through high-interest accounts.

The goal isn't to deprive yourself but to align your spending with your values and long-term objectives. By implementing these strategies, you save money and invest in your future self. So, start small, stay consistent, and watch your savings grow.

Most importantly, be patient with yourself. Building strong saving habits takes time, and there may be setbacks along the way. That's okay! Every step towards better saving habits is a step towards a more secure financial future.

BUILDING AN EMERGENCY FUND

Life has a knack for surprises, doesn't it? One moment, you're sailing smoothly, feeling on top of your finances, and the next – wham! Your car breaks down, your roof springs a leak, or an unexpected medical bill lands in your mailbox. These curveballs are where your emergency fund steps in, playing the role of your financial superhero.

Think of an emergency fund as your personal financial safety net. It's a stash of money set aside specifically for those 'uh-oh' moments in life. We're talking about genuine emergencies – unexpected medical bills, surprise car repairs, or even job loss. It's not for that new smartphone you've been eyeing or your annual vacation – it's strictly for when life throws you a financial curveball.

Why is an Emergency Fund Crucial?

1. Stress Reducer: Knowing you have a financial cushion can significantly lower your stress levels when unexpected expenses arise.

2. Debt Preventer: Without an emergency fund, you might be forced to rely on credit cards or loans to cover unexpected costs, potentially leading to a cycle of debt.

3. Freedom Provider: An emergency fund gives you the power to make decisions based on what's best for you, not just what you can afford at the moment.

4. Opportunity Creator: Sometimes, an emergency can be an opportunity in disguise. With an emergency fund, you're better positioned to take advantage of these situations.

How Much Should You Save?

The general rule of thumb is to save enough to cover 3-6 months of living expenses. But let's break this down a bit:

- If you're single and have a stable job, aim for 3 months of expenses.
- If you have dependents or a variable income, Shoot for 6 months or more.

To calculate your target amount, follow these steps:

1. List all your essential monthly expenses (rent, utilities, food, transportation, etc.).
2. Add them up to get your monthly essential spending.
3. Multiply this number by 3 (or 6, depending on your situation).

For example, if your monthly essentials total $2,000, your emergency fund goal would be between $6,000 (3 months) and $12,000 (6 months).

Where to Keep Your Emergency Fund

Now that you're saving, let's make sure your money is working as hard as possible for you, especially regarding your emergency fund. While the primary purpose of an emergency fund is to provide a financial safety net, that doesn't mean it can't earn some interest along the way. Let's explore some smart options that balance accessibility with growth potential.

Your emergency fund must be easily accessible but not so accessible that you're tempted to dip into it for non-emergencies. This delicate balance can be achieved through a few different account types, each with its own advantages.

- High-yield Savings Accounts
- Money Market Account
- Certificates of Deposit

High-yield Savings Accounts are an excellent option for emergency funds. These accounts are similar to regular savings but offer significantly higher interest rates. Typically offered by online banks with lower overhead costs, these accounts can pass those savings on to customers through higher interest rates. While a traditional brick-and-mortar bank might offer an interest rate of 0.01% on a savings account, a high-yield savings account could offer 1% or more rates. This difference may seem small, but it can add up over time, allowing your emergency fund to grow faster while being readily available when needed.

Money Market Accounts is another option to consider. These accounts are similar to savings accounts but often come with higher interest rates and the ability to write checks. This added flexibility can be useful in emergencies where you need to access your funds quickly. However, it's important to note that money market accounts may have higher minimum balance requirements than standard savings accounts.

Certificates of Deposit, or CDs, are savings options that often provide higher interest rates than traditional savings accounts. When you open a CD, you agree to leave your money untouched for a specific period, known as the term. Terms can range from a few months to several years, and generally, the longer the term, the higher the interest rate. While CDs typically offer higher rates, they come with a caveat: your money is locked in for the term of the CD, and early withdrawal usually results in penalties.

However, there's a strategy that can make CDs more suitable for emergency funds: the CD ladder. This involves spreading your money across multiple CDs with different maturity dates. For example, you might put some money in a 3-month CD, some in a 6-month CD, and some in a 9-month CD. As each CD matures, you can either withdraw the money if needed or reinvest it in a new CD. This approach gives you higher interest rates and periodic access to your funds.

When choosing between these options, it's crucial to remember the primary purpose of your emergency fund. While earning interest is a nice bonus, the main goals are liquidity and safety. Your emergency fund isn't an investment – it's insurance against life's unexpected events. You need to be able to access this money quickly and without penalty when emergencies arise.

For this reason, keeping the bulk of your emergency fund in a high-yield savings account is recommended. This option provides a good balance of accessibility, safety, and modest growth. You might consider keeping a portion in a money market account for even quicker access and possibly using a CD ladder for a part of your fund if you have a larger emergency fund.

Maintaining Your Emergency Fund

Congratulations! You've built up your emergency fund. But remember, this is just the beginning. Maintaining your emergency fund is just as crucial as building it. Here's how to keep your financial safety net strong and ready:

- **Replenish After Use:** Life happens, and you might need to dip into your fund. That's okay – it's what it's there for. However, make it a priority to replenish your funds as soon as possible. Treat it like any other important bill that needs to be paid.

- **Stay Vigilant with Regular Reviews:** Your life isn't static, nor should your emergency fund be. As your circumstances change – perhaps you've gotten a raise, started a family, or moved to a new city – your emergency fund needs may change too. Set a reminder to review your fund annually and adjust it as necessary.
- **Keep it Sacred and Separate:** Resist the temptation to dip into your emergency fund for non-emergencies by keeping it in a separate account. This clear boundary helps reinforce the importance of your fund and makes it less likely you'll use it impulsively.
- **Embrace Continuous Growth:** Even after reaching your initial goal, consider continuing to grow your fund. The more robust your safety net, the more peace of mind you'll have. A larger fund can help you weather longer periods of financial stress or bigger emergencies.

Following these maintenance strategies will ensure your emergency fund remains a strong, reliable safety net, ready to catch you when life throws its inevitable curveballs.

Common Emergency Fund Mistakes to Avoid

As you build and maintain your emergency fund, you must be aware of potential pitfalls. Here are some common mistakes to avoid:

1. Using It for Non-Emergencies: It's tempting to dip into your emergency fund for non-essential purchases. That amazing sale at your favorite store or the latest tech gadget isn't an emergency. Neither are planned expenses like weddings or vacations. Stay disciplined and keep your emergency fund for true emergencies only.

2. Keeping It in Your Checking Account: Mixing your emergency fund with your everyday spending money increases the temptation to use it impulsively. Keep your emergency fund separate to maintain a clear boundary between your safety net and your regular finances.

3. Investing It in Volatile Assets: While it might be tempting to try to grow your emergency fund quickly, investing it in stocks, ETFs, or mutual funds is risky. These investments can lose value rapidly, and you might be unable to access your money quickly when needed. Your emergency fund should be in safe, liquid options like high-yield savings accounts or money market funds. Remember, the primary goal of your emergency fund is security and accessibility, not high returns.

4. Neglecting to Replenish: Life happens, and you might need to use your emergency fund. That's what it's there for! However, make sure you plan to build it back up as soon as possible. Treat replenishing your emergency fund as a top financial priority.

5. Setting It and Forgetting It: Your emergency fund needs may change as your life circumstances evolve. Regularly review and adjust your fund size. Did you get a raise? Have a child? Move to a more expensive area? These life changes might necessitate a larger emergency fund.

6. Thinking of It as an Investment: Your emergency fund is not an investment vehicle. It's a form of insurance against life's unexpected events. Once you have a solid emergency fund and additional savings, you can start thinking about investing for growth. We'll dive deeper into investment strategies in the next book, but for now, focus on building and maintaining your financial safety net.

Remember, your emergency fund is your financial first line of defense. By avoiding these common mistakes, you'll ensure it's there when you truly need it, providing you with peace of mind and financial stability in the face of life's uncertainties.

Building an emergency fund isn't always easy. It requires discipline, patience, and sometimes sacrifice. But the peace of mind it provides is priceless. Imagine facing a sudden, expensive car repair and being able to say, 'No problem, I've got this covered.' That's the power of an emergency fund.

Think of it as a gift to your future self. Every dollar you save is a little stress relief you're banking for later.

As we conclude our exploration of saving strategies, it's time to see how these techniques fit into the bigger picture of your finances. Saving is crucial but most effective when part of a comprehensive plan. In the next chapter, "The Basics of Budgeting," we'll learn how to create a financial roadmap incorporating your new saving habits while guiding all aspects of your money management. Get ready to discover how saving and budgeting work in tandem to accelerate your path to financial success!

CHAPTER 3
THE BASICS OF BUDGETING

UNDERSTANDING INCOME AND EXPENSES

Have you ever set out on a road trip without a map or GPS? Probably not. You'd likely plan your route, figure out your pit stops, and estimate your expenses before hitting the road. That's precisely what a budget does for your financial journey. It's your fiscal roadmap, guiding you through the twists and turns of your financial life. And just like a well-planned trip can be an adventure rather than a stress-fest, a well-crafted budget can transform your relationship with money from anxiety-inducing to empowering.

Welcome to the world of budgeting, where we'll turn those vague money worries into a clear, actionable plan. Don't worry if the word 'budget' makes you want to run for the hills -- I promise, by the end of this section, you'll see budgeting as your financial superpower, not a boring chore.

What Exactly is a Budget?

Let's start with the basics. A budget is simply a plan for your money. It's a tool that helps you understand how much money you have coming in, where it's going, and how you can direct it toward your goals. Think of it as a roadmap for your finances -- it shows you where you are, where you want to go, and how to get there.

But why is budgeting so important? Well, imagine losing weight without ever stepping on a scale or tracking what you eat. You might make some progress, but you'd have no real way of knowing how you're doing or how to improve. Budgeting does for your finances what a scale and food diary do for your health -- it gives you awareness and control.

Show Me the Money: Understanding Your Income

Before creating a budget, we need to know how much money we're working with. This means identifying all your sources of income. For many of you, this might simply be your regular salary from your 9-to-5 job. But don't stop there! Consider other potential sources: freelance or gig work (did you design a logo for your cousin's new business? That counts!), investment income, or even that $20 bill you found in your old jeans.

Once you've identified all your income sources, it's time to calculate your net income. This is the amount you have available to spend after taxes and other deductions. It's important to use your net income when budgeting, not your gross income (the amount before deductions). Using your gross income is like counting your chickens before they hatch -- it'll lead to over-spending and frustration.

Where Does It All Go? Understanding Your Expenses

Now that we know how much money is coming in, let's look at where it's going. Expenses generally fall into three categories:

- **Fixed expenses:** These are costs that stay relatively constant month to month, like rent or mortgage payments, car payments, or insurance premiums.
- **Variable expenses:** These costs can fluctuate from month to month. Think groceries, utilities, or gas for your car.
- **Discretionary expenses:** This is the fun stuff – eating out, entertainment, new clothes, etc. These are typically the easiest expenses to cut if you need to tighten your belt.

Understanding these categories is crucial because it helps you identify where you have the most control over your spending. While you might not be able to change your rent overnight, you can probably find ways to reduce your grocery bill or cut back on dining out.

The Money Trail: Tracking Your Income and Expenses

Now comes the part many people dread, but I promise it's not as bad as you think. Tracking your income and expenses is like being a detective in your own financial mystery. You're gathering clues about where your money comes from and where it goes. This exercise isn't about restriction; it's about awareness. You might be surprised where your money is actually going. Are those small daily purchases adding up more than you realized? Is there a category where you're spending more than you thought? This snapshot will give you valuable insights into your spending habits.

For the next month, I challenge you to track every single penny you spend. Yes, every single penny. That morning coffee, the impulse buys at the checkout line, the subscription you forgot you had -- write it all down. Use a notebook, spreadsheet, or budgeting app -- whatever works for you. At the end of the month, categorize your expenses and total them up. This might seem tedious, but I promise it's eye-opening. Most people are shocked when they see where their money actually goes.

How to Track Expenses Effectively:

- **Choose Your Method:** Use a notebook, spreadsheet, or budgeting app. The key is to choose a method you're comfortable with and will use consistently.
- **Record Everything:** No expense is too small to track. That $2 vending machine snack or $5 coffee all add up over time.
- **Categorize Your Expenses:** Group your expenses into categories like housing, transportation, food, entertainment, etc. This makes it easier to analyze your spending patterns.
- **Be Consistent:** Make expense tracking a daily habit. Set aside a few minutes each day to record your expenses while they're fresh in your mind.
- **Use Technology:** Many banks offer categorization features in their online banking platforms. Budgeting apps like Mint or YNAB can automatically import and categorize your transactions, making the process even easier.
- **Review Regularly:** Review your expenses at the end of each week or month. Look for patterns, surprises, and areas where you might be able to cut back.

The 30-Day Challenge: Your Financial Eye-Opener

Here's where the rubber meets the road. I challenge you to track every single penny you spend for the next 30 days. Yes, every single penny. That morning coffee, the impulse buys at the checkout line, the subscription you forgot you had – write it all down.

- For one month, track every single expense, no matter how small.
- At the end of the month, categorize your expenses and total them up.
- Analyze your spending. Are you surprised by any categories? Are you spending in line with your priorities and goals?
- Use this information to create or adjust your budget.

This might seem tedious, but I promise it's eye-opening. Most people are shocked when they see where their money actually goes. You might discover you're spending $100 monthly on subscriptions you barely use or that your "occasional" takeout habit is costing you more than your grocery bill.

Remember, the goal of tracking expenses isn't to make you feel guilty about your spending. It's about gaining knowledge and control over your finances. By understanding where your money goes, you're taking the first crucial step towards achieving your financial goals.

Once you've tracked your spending for a month, it's time to play financial detective. Look for patterns in your spending. Are there certain times of the month when you tend to spend more? Do you notice any emotional spending triggers?

But it's not all about cutting back. This analysis can also help you recognize opportunities for saving. Could you redirect some of that coffee shop money into your savings account? Or maybe you could find a cheaper alternative for one of your subscriptions?

Remember, the goal here isn't to eliminate all fun from your life. It's about making conscious choices about where your money goes so you can align your spending with your values and goals.

Bringing It All Together

Understanding your income and expenses is the foundation of good budgeting. It's like taking a financial selfie – it shows you exactly where you stand right now. And just like a selfie, it might not always be flattering, but it's real.

You've taken the crucial first steps toward financial control by identifying all your income sources, categorizing your expenses, and tracking your spending. You now have the information you need to make informed decisions about your money.

In the next section, we'll use this information to create your first budget. But for now, pat yourself on the back. You've already done something many people never do – you've faced your financial reality head-on. And trust me, that's no small feat.

Remember, budgeting isn't about restriction; it's about freedom. It's about making your money work for you instead of the other way around. So, take a deep breath and prepare for the next step in your financial journey. You've got this!

CREATING YOUR FIRST BUDGET

Alright, you've done the groundwork. You've tracked your income and expenses, and you're starting to get a clear picture of your financial landscape. Now it's time for the main event: creating your first budget. Don't worry if that sounds daunting -- I promise, by the end of this section, you'll be ready to craft a budget that works for you, not against you. Remember, a budget isn't a financial straitjacket; it's a tool that gives you control and helps you align your spending with your goals and values.

Before we dive into the nuts and bolts of budgeting, let's talk about goals. After all, a budget without goals is like a ship without a destination -- you might be moving, but you're not going anywhere. Financial goals come in two flavors: short-term and long-term. Short-term goals might include saving for a vacation, buying a new laptop, or paying off a small debt. These are the goals that keep you motivated day-to-day. Long-term goals, however, are your big-picture aspirations -- buying a house, retiring comfortably, or starting your own business.

But here's the key: your goals need to be SMART. As we have already discussed in Chapter 2, that stands for Specific, Measurable, Achievable, Relevant, and Time-bound. Instead of saying, 'I want to save money,' a SMART goal would be, 'I want to save $5,000 for a down payment on a car in 18 months.' Setting SMART goals gives your budget purpose and direction. It turns vague wishes into concrete targets, making staying motivated and tracking progress easier.

Choosing Your Budgeting Method

Now that we've got our goals, it's time to choose a budgeting method. Think of this like choosing a diet – there's no one-size-fits-all solution. The best method is the one you'll actually stick to. Let's look at a few popular options:

- **The 50/30/20 Rule:** This method suggests allocating 50% of your income to needs, 30% to wants, and 20%

to savings and debt repayment. It's simple and flexible, making it great for beginners.

- **Zero-Based Budgeting:** You assign every dollar to a job using this method. Your income minus your expenses (including savings) should equal zero. It's more time-intensive but gives you maximum control over your money.
- **Envelope System:** This old-school method involves putting cash for different expense categories into physical envelopes. When an envelope is empty, you're done spending in that category for the month. It's great for visual learners and overspends.
- **Pay Yourself First:** With this method, you prioritize savings and investing before allocating money to other expenses. It's excellent for aggressive savers but requires discipline with the remaining funds.

Creating Your Budget

Now, let's roll up our sleeves and create that budget. Don't worry – we'll take it step by step.

1. **Calculate Your Total Income:** Remember when we identified all your income sources? Add them up to get your total monthly income.
2. **List All Expenses:** Use the information from your expense tracking to list all your regular expenses.
3. **Categorize Expenses:** Group your expenses into categories like housing, transportation, food, etc. This makes it easier to analyze your spending.
4. **Allocate Funds to Each Category:** Based on your chosen budgeting method, allocate your income to each expense category. Don't forget to include savings as a category!

5. **Balance the Budget:** Ensure your total expenses (including savings) don't exceed your income. If they do, it's time to make tough decisions about where to cut back.

Remember, your first budget probably won't be perfect, and that's okay. Budgeting is a skill, and like any skill, it takes practice to master.

Real-Life Budget Templates: Adapting to Different Income Levels and Life Stages

To help you create a budget that fits your unique financial situation, we've prepared three real-life budget templates based on different income levels and life stages. These examples demonstrate applying the budgeting methods we discussed earlier, providing practical, adaptable frameworks for your financial planning. Whether you're just starting your career, managing a family, or dealing with variable income, these templates offer valuable insights into effective money management strategies. Feel free to use these as starting points, adjusting the numbers and categories to align with your personal financial goals and circumstances.

Case 1: Sarah, Entry-Level Marketer
Income: $35,000/year (Monthly: $2,917)
Strategy: **50/30/20 budget**

50% Needs ($1,458):

- Rent (shared apartment): $700
- Utilities: $150
- Groceries: $300
- Transportation: $200

- Health insurance: $108

30% Wants ($875):

- Travel fund: $300
- Entertainment: $200
- Dining out: $150
- Shopping: $125
- Gym membership: $100

20% Savings ($584):

- 401(k) contribution (with employer match): $334
- Emergency fund: $250

This breakdown allows Sarah to maintain a balanced budget while prioritizing her travel goals and building financial security through retirement savings and an emergency fund.

Case 2: Michael & Lisa, Mid-Career Couple with Kids
Combined Income: $120,000/year (Monthly: $10,000)
Strategy: **Zero-based budget**

- Mortgage: $2,500/month
- Utilities: $400/month
- Groceries: $800/month
- Transportation: $600/month
- Insurance: $500/month
- Debt payments: $1,000/month
- Retirement savings: $1,500/month
- Kids' college fund: $500/month
- Sinking funds (car repairs, holidays): $700/month
- Entertainment: $400/month
- Miscellaneous: $600/month

- Emergency fund: $500/month

Total: $10,000/month

Every dollar has a job, with sinking funds for irregular expenses and automated savings for long-term goals. This approach ensures all income is allocated purposefully, aligning spending with priorities and financial objectives.

Case 3: Amelia, Freelance Graphic Designer
Average Income: $60,000/year (Monthly average: $5,000, but variable)
Strategy: **Percentage-based budget** with a large buffer

Based on the lowest-earning month ($3,500):

- Essential expenses (50%): $1,750 (Rent: $1,000, Utilities: $200, Groceries: $350, Insurance: $200)
- Taxes and business expenses (25%): $875
- Savings and debt repayment (15%): $525 (Emergency fund: $300, Retirement: $225)
- Discretionary spending (10%): $350

During high-income months, excess funds are allocated:

- Additional savings (50% of excess)
- Business reinvestment (30% of excess)
- "Fun money" (20% of excess)

This approach ensures Amelia can cover essentials and save consistently while capitalizing on higher-earning periods.

These cases demonstrate that effective budgeting is possible at any income level – it's all about aligning your money with your priorities and preparing for the future. Whether you're an entry-level employee, a mid-career couple with kids, or a freelancer with variable income, these examples can serve as templates for creating your own budget.

Feel free to adjust the percentages and categories to fit your unique financial situation and goals. The key is to find a budgeting method that works for you and stick to it consistently.

Adapting Your Budget: The Art of Financial Flexibility

Creating a budget is just the first step. The real key to long-term success lies in adapting and adjusting your budget as your life evolves. Your budget should be a living document that grows and changes with you, reflecting the dynamic nature of your financial life.

Life is unpredictable, and your financial situation can change in the blink of an eye. A promotion at work, a new addition to the family, or an unexpected medical expense can all dramatically alter your financial landscape. That's why regularly reviewing and adjusting your budget is crucial. Set aside time each month to assess your budget's performance. Are you staying on track with your goals? Where did you overspend? Where did you have extra? Use these insights to refine your budget for the coming month.

As you go through major life changes – a new job, a move to a new city, or a growing family – your budget will need more significant adjustments. Don't be afraid to overhaul your budget if necessary completely. Your financial plan should work for you, not the other way around. If you find yourself consistently overspending in certain categories, it might be time to reassess your allocations. Be honest with yourself about your needs and wants and adjust accordingly.

Remember to account for seasonal fluctuations in your budget as well. Your heating bill might skyrocket in winter, or you might spend more on social activities in summer. A good budget anticipates these predictable changes. Consider creating separate budget templates for different seasons or allocating funds to a "seasonal expenses" category that you can draw from as needed.

As your income grows, resist the temptation to inflate your lifestyle immediately. Instead, use this as an opportunity to supercharge your financial goals. Could you increase your debt payments? Boost your savings rate? Or, finally, start that investment portfolio you've been dreaming about? Make conscious decisions about how to allocate any increase in income.

Don't forget to adjust your financial goals along with your budget. As your life circumstances change, your short-term and long-term financial objectives may also need to shift. Maybe that dream vacation fund needs to become a baby fund, or your retirement timeline has changed. Regular "big picture" reviews of your financial goals ensure your budget always aligns with what matters most.

Lastly, be kind to yourself during this process. Budgeting is a skill that improves with time and practice. If you find that you've veered off course, don't beat yourself up. Instead, view it as valuable data that can help you create a more realistic and sustainable budget moving forward. Remember, the goal isn't perfection – it's progress.

Riding the Income Roller Coaster: Budgeting for Irregular Income

If you're a freelancer, gig worker, or have a commission-based job, budgeting can want to try to hit a moving target. But don't worry – you can still create a stable financial foundation.

The key is creating a "salary" based on your lowest-earning months. Any income above this goes into savings or towards extra debt payments. This approach helps smooth out the feast-or-famine cycle many irregular earners experience.

Prioritizing expenses becomes crucial when your income fluctuates. Make a list of your essential expenses that keep a roof over your head and food on the table. These get paid first. Everything else comes after.

Lastly, build a larger emergency fund. Aim for 6-12 months of expenses rather than the standard 3-6 months. This extra buffer can help you weather periods of low income without stress.

Avoiding the Pitfalls: Common Budgeting Mistakes

Even the most diligent budgeters can fall into some common traps. Here are a few to watch out for:

- **Unrealistic Expectations:** Don't expect to be a budgeting pro overnight. Finding a system that works for you and changing long-standing habits takes time.
- **Forgetting Irregular Expenses:** Don't forget about those expenses that only come up once or twice a year, like car registration or holiday gifts. Budget for these in advance to avoid surprises.
- **Not Budgeting for Savings and Emergencies:** Savings isn't what's left over at the end of the month – it should be a priority in your budget.
- **Trying to Be Too Perfect:** Your budget is a guideline, not a straitjacket. Don't beat yourself up if you go over in one category occasionally. The goal is progress, not perfection.

Budgeting as a Team: Involving Partners or Roommates

Navigating the financial landscape together becomes crucial when sharing expenses with a partner or roommates. Money discussions can be sensitive, but open and honest communication forms the bedrock of successful financial teamwork. Regular conversations about financial goals, concerns, and spending habits help create a shared understanding and prevent misunderstandings down the line.

Establishing a clear division of expenses is essential. While there's no one-size-fits-all approach, everyone must agree on the system. Some may opt for a 50/50 split, while others might divide expenses based on income proportions. Whatever method you choose, ensure it feels fair and sustainable for all parties involved.

While working towards shared financial goals is important, maintaining individual financial autonomy can prevent resentment and promote independence. Consider allocating a portion of the budget as "no questions asked" money for each person. This allows for personal spending without scrutiny, fostering a balance between teamwork and individual freedom.

Utilizing technology can streamline the process of shared expenses. Apps like Splitwise, SettleUp, or Tricount are designed to split costs among roommates or partners. These tools can help avoid arguments by keeping clear records and ensuring everyone pays their fair share.

Remember, financial compatibility doesn't necessitate identical views on money. It's about finding a system that respects everyone's financial values and works for the group as a whole. This might involve compromises and adjustments along the way. Regular check-ins can help ensure the system remains effective and fair as circumstances change.

Consider creating a shared budget for common expenses while maintaining separate accounts for personal spending. This approach can help balance shared responsibilities with individual financial freedom. It's also wise to discuss long-term financial goals as a team, even if you're roommates. Understanding each other's financial aspirations can lead to more supportive and harmonious living arrangements.

Successful financial teamwork is built on trust, transparency, and flexibility. By approaching money matters as a team, you can create a strong financial foundation that supports your shared living arrangement and individual financial well-being.

TOOLS AND APPS TO SIMPLIFY BUDGETING

Alright, budget warriors, you've set your goals, chosen your method, and created your first budget. Give yourself a pat on the back -- you're already miles ahead of most people regarding financial management. But let's face it: in today's digital age, why make things harder than necessary? It's time to bring your budgeting game into the 21st century with nifty tools and apps that can make the whole process much easier (and, dare I say, even a little fun?).

The Budgeting Toolbox:

Before diving into the world of budgeting apps, let's take a quick tour of the different budgeting tools at your disposal. Spreadsheets are the OG of budgeting tools. Programs like Microsoft Excel and Google Sheets offer a blank canvas for creating a custom budgeting system. They're incredibly flexible and powerful but require some knowledge and effort to set up. Mobile apps are the cool kids on the block. Budgeting apps on your smartphone put your financial management literally at your fingertips. They often come with features like automatic transaction importing and categorization, making it easy to stay on top of your budget on the go. Desktop software sits in the middle ground between spreadsheets and mobile apps. They offer more features than a basic spreadsheet but may provide more detailed analysis tools than a mobile app.

Let's zoom in on some of the most popular budgeting apps. Remember, there's no one-size-fits-all solution – the best app for you is the one you'll actually use consistently.

Tools and Apps to Simplify Budgeting

In today's digital age, numerous tools and apps can simplify the budgeting process, making it easier to track your spending, set financial goals, and stay on top of your finances. Let's explore some popular options and how they can enhance your budgeting experience.

Mint: This free app automatically imports and categorizes transactions from linked bank accounts and credit cards. It offers a comprehensive overview of your finances, including bill reminders and credit score tracking. Mint is ideal for those who want a hands-off approach to expense tracking.

YNAB (You Need A Budget): Based on the zero-based budgeting method, YNAB requires more hands-on interaction but can be highly effective for those who want to be more intentional with their spending. It encourages you to give every dollar a job and offers educational resources to improve your financial habits.

Personal Capital: While it offers budgeting features, its strength lies in investment tracking and analysis. It's an excellent choice for those looking to budget and grow their wealth through investments.

Goodbudget: This app brings the envelope budgeting system into the digital world. It's particularly useful for couples who want to share a budget and those who prefer a more tactile approach to money management.

Spreadsheet Templates: For those who prefer more control and customization, spreadsheet programs like Microsoft Excel or Google Sheets can be powerful budgeting tools. Many pre-made budgeting templates are available online, or you can create your own to suit your specific needs.

When selecting a budgeting tool, several factors should be considered. First, consider the ease of use -- look for an interface that you find intuitive and enjoyable to interact with. This will increase the likelihood of you using the tool consistently. Next, evaluate the features offered by each tool. Ensure it provides the required functionalities like bill reminders, goal tracking, or investment monitoring. Security is another crucial aspect to consider. Prioritize apps with strong encryption and two-factor authentication to safeguard sensitive financial data. Finally, weigh the cost against the features provided. While many apps offer free versions, some require a subscription for full functionality. Determine which option provides the best value for your specific needs.

Choosing Your Perfect Match: Tips for Picking the Right Budgeting Tool

Alright, so you've got the lay of the land regarding budgeting tools. But how do you choose the right one for you? Here are some factors to consider:

- **Tech-Savviness:** Be honest with yourself. Are you a tech wizard, or does the thought of a new app make you break out in a cold sweat? If you're not super tech-savvy, look for apps with simple interfaces and good customer support.

- **Budgeting Needs:** Think about what you really need from a budgeting tool. Are you just starting and need something simple? Or are you looking for an in-depth investment analysis? Choose a tool that aligns with your financial goals and budgeting style.
- **Cost vs. Features:** While great free options exist, don't dismiss paid apps outright. Sometimes, the features and support you get with a paid app can be well worth the cost if it helps you save more in the long run.
- **Try Before You Buy:** Most paid apps offer free trials. Take advantage of these to test-drive different apps and see which one feels right for you.
- **Read User Reviews:** Other users can offer valuable insights into the pros and cons of different apps. Just remember to take reviews with a grain of salt – what works for someone else might not work for you.

Integrating Technology with Traditional Methods

Now, I know some of you might be thinking, "But I like my old-school budgeting method. Do I have to give that up?" Not at all! In fact, some of the most effective budgeting strategies combine traditional methods with modern technology.

Remember, these tools are meant to make your life easier, not more complicated. If you spend hours fiddling with an app or stressing over categories, it might be time to simplify your approach. The goal is to find a system that works for you and that you'll stick with in the long term. Maybe that means using an app for tracking expenses but still sitting down with pen and paper at the end of each month to review and plan. Or perhaps you use a budgeting app for the heavy lifting but keep a simple spreadsheet for your long-term financial goals.

The key is to leverage technology to support your budgeting efforts, not to let it become another source of financial stress. With the right tools in your arsenal, you'll be well-equipped to keep your budget on track and your financial goals within reach.

REPAYING DEBT AND BUDGETING FOR LIFE EVENTS

Life's financial landscape is dotted with both obstacles and landmarks. This section will explore two critical aspects of managing your money: conquering debt and preparing for significant life events. We'll begin by tackling the weight of debt head-on, starting with creating a debt repayment budget that aligns with your financial goals and personality. Whether you're drawn to the quick wins of the Debt Snowball method or the mathematical efficiency of the Debt Avalanche approach, we'll help you craft a strategy to lighten your financial load and pave the way for future success.

Creating a Debt Repayment Budget

Debt can feel like a heavy backpack weighing you down on your financial journey. But with the right strategy, you can lighten that load and eventually cast it off entirely.

Start by listing all your debts, including the balance, interest rate, and minimum payment for each. This gives you a clear picture of what you're dealing with. Generally, you'll want to focus on high-interest debt first, as it's costing you the most money over time.

Two popular methods stand out in tackling debt: Debt Snowball and Debt Avalanche. Each approach has its merits, and the best choice depends on your personal financial situation and psychological tendencies.

The Debt Snowball method, popularized by financial guru Dave Ramsey, focuses on paying off your smallest debt first, regardless of interest rates. After making minimum payments on all debts, you funnel any extra money into the smallest balance. Once that's paid off, you roll the amount you were paying on that debt into the next smallest, creating a "snowball" effect. The psychological boost from quickly eliminating smaller debts can be incredibly motivating, helping you build momentum and stay committed to your debt repayment journey.

Let's say you have the following debts:

Credit Card A: $1,000 balance, 15% interest
Personal Loan: $3,000 balance, 10% interest
Credit Card B: $5,000 balance, 18% interest
Using the Debt Snowball method, you'd pay them off in this order:
Credit Card A ($1,000)
Personal Loan ($3,000)
Credit Card B ($5,000)

The Debt Avalanche method prioritizes debts with the highest interest rates. Mathematically, this approach saves you the most money in interest over time. By tackling high-interest debts first, you reduce the overall amount you'll pay and potentially get out of debt faster. This method appeals to those who prefer a more logical, numbers-driven approach to personal finance.

Recent studies have shown that while the Avalanche method is mathematically superior, the Snowball method often leads to higher rates of debt elimination. A 2016 Journal of Consumer Research study found that people pursuing the Snowball method were more likely to eliminate their entire debt load.

Using the same debts as the example before:

Credit Card A: $1,000 balance, 15% interest
Personal Loan: $3,000 balance, 10% interest
Credit Card B: $5,000 balance, 18% interest
With the Debt Avalanche method, you'd pay them off in this order:
Credit Card B ($5,000 at 18% interest)
Credit Card A ($1,000 at 15% interest)
Personal Loan ($3,000 at 10% interest)

Ultimately, the best method is the one you'll stick to consistently. Some people even opt for a hybrid approach, starting with the Snowball to build motivation and then switching to the Avalanche to maximize savings. Whatever method you choose, the key is to stay committed and celebrate every victory.

Treat debt repayment as a non-negotiable expense in your budget. Start by making the minimum payments on all debts, then allocate any extra money towards your target debt (the smallest balance or the highest interest rate, depending on your chosen method). Remember, every extra dollar you put towards debt gets you closer to financial freedom.

Budgeting for Life Events

Life is a journey filled with twists, turns, and unexpected detours. While we can't predict every bump in the road, we can certainly prepare for the big milestones and transitions that most of us will face. Let's explore how to adapt your budget for these significant life events and long-term goals. Think of it as financial map-making for the major landmarks of your life.

Moving Out on Your Own:

Ah, the sweet taste of independence! But before you start picking out curtains for your new place, let's talk numbers. Moving out means a whole new set of expenses: rent, utilities, groceries, and maybe even renter's insurance. Start by researching the cost of living in your desired area. Don't forget to factor in one-time costs like security deposits and moving expenses.

Build up a "moving fund" in the months leading up to your move. Aim for at least three months' worth of expenses to give yourself a financial cushion.

Starting a New Job:

Congrats on the new gig! A new job often means a change in income, but don't fall into the lifestyle inflation trap. If you're earning more, resist the urge to upgrade your lifestyle immediately. Instead, use this opportunity to boost your savings or pay down debt.

Remember to account for any changes in benefits. Maybe your new job offers better health insurance, or you must budget for a longer commute. Don't forget about retirement contributions – if your new employer offers a 401(k) match, try to contribute enough to get the full match. It's essentially free money! (We will learn more about 401(k) later in this section).

Buying a Car

When budgeting for a car, remember to factor in all the associated costs: insurance, gas, maintenance, and parking. Determine how much you can afford to spend monthly on transportation.

If you're financing the car, aim to put down at least 20% to avoid being "underwater" on your loan (owing more than the car is worth). And remember, just because a dealer says you qualify for a certain monthly payment doesn't mean it fits your budget!

Down Payment on a House

Buying a house is often the biggest purchase most people make. Start by determining how much house you can afford and what size down payment you'll need. Conventional wisdom suggests aiming for a 20% down payment to avoid private mortgage insurance, but there are options for lower down payments.

Create a separate savings account for your down payment fund and set up automatic transfers to it each month. Consider cutting back on discretionary expenses or picking up a side hustle to accelerate your savings.

Having a Baby:

Parenthood is an adventure; like any good adventure, it requires preparation. Start by researching the costs of having a baby – from medical expenses to diapers and childcare. Consider setting up a "baby fund" to cover initial expenses if you plan.

Your budget must accommodate ongoing costs like childcare, health insurance, and, eventually, education savings. Don't forget to factor in any changes to your income if you or your partner plan to take parental leave or reduce work hours.

Retirement Planning: Securing Your Financial Future

When managing your money and planning your future, it is important to zoom out and consider the ultimate financial milestone: retirement. I know what you're thinking - retirement seems like a far-off concept, especially if you're starting your career or in the thick of raising a family. But trust me, your future self will be incredibly grateful if you start planning now.

When it comes to retirement savings, time truly is your superpower. The magic of compound interest means that even modest contributions can snowball into substantial sums over the decades. Let me illustrate this with a real-world example: if you start tucking away $200 monthly at age 25, assuming a 7% annual return, you could sit on a nest egg of over $500,000 by age 65. But if you wait until 35 to start the same savings plan, you'd end up with less than half that amount. It's a stark reminder that when it comes to retirement planning, the early bird really does catch the worm.

So, how much should you aim to save? A good rule of thumb is to squirrel away 10-15% of your income for retirement. That might sound daunting, especially when juggling student loans and rent and maybe dreaming of a home purchase. But here's a pro tip: if your employer offers a 401(k) match, make it your mission to contribute enough to snag that full match. It's essentially free money - like finding a $20 bill in your jacket pocket, but potentially worth thousands over time.

A 401(k) plan is a retirement savings account sponsored by an employer. It's named after the U.S. Internal Revenue Code section that established it. Here's a breakdown of how it works:

- **Contributions:** Employees can have a portion of their

paycheck automatically deposited into their 401(k) account before taxes are taken out.

- **Employer Match:** Many companies offer to match a percentage of the employee's contributions, essentially providing free money towards retirement savings.
- **Tax Benefits:** Contributions are made with pre-tax dollars, reducing your annual taxable income. The money in the account grows tax-deferred until withdrawal.

Now, let's talk strategy. Treat your retirement contributions like any other non-negotiable expense in your budget. Just as you wouldn't skip your rent payment, prioritize your retirement contribution. Can't hit that 10-15% target right away? No worries. Start with what you can and gradually increase your contributions. Even a 1% yearly increase can make a significant difference over time.

While we're on the subject of retirement accounts, let's quickly break down your options. Beyond the 401(k), consider opening an Individual Retirement Account (IRA). There are two main types: Traditional and Roth. The key difference lies in when you pay taxes.

- Traditional IRA: you get a tax break now and pay taxes when you withdraw in retirement.
- Roth IRA flips the script - you pay taxes now, but your retirement withdrawal is tax-free.

Your choice depends on your current tax situation and where you think you'll be in retirement.

I'd be remiss if I didn't address a common concern: balancing retirement savings with other financial goals. Yes, retirement is crucial, but it's not your only priority. You're also likely eyeing debt repayment, building an emergency fund, or saving for a home. The key is to find a balance that works for you.

Remember that retirement planning is the ultimate long game. It requires patience, consistency, and a bit of faith in your future self. But by starting early and making retirement savings a habit, you're setting yourself up for a future where financial stress takes a backseat to enjoying your golden years. So, whether retirement for you means traveling the world, spoiling grandkids, or simply enjoying a well-deserved rest, the steps you take today are paving the way for that vision to become a reality.

CHAPTER 4
UNDERSTANDING CREDIT

HOW CREDIT SCORES WORK

Now that you've mastered budgeting, you're ready to tackle another crucial aspect of personal finance: credit. A solid budget isn't just about managing your current money—it's also about preparing for future financial moves. Understanding and using credit wisely is a natural next step in your financial journey. Your budgeting skills will be a strong foundation for responsible credit use, helping you make informed decisions about when and how to leverage credit to your advantage. Let's dive into the world of credit!

You've probably heard the term "credit score" thrown around quite a bit, especially if you've ever tried to rent an apartment, apply for a loan, or even get a new cell phone plan. But what exactly is this mysterious number, and why does it seem to have so much power over our financial lives? Let's dive in and demystify the world of credit scores.

What is a Credit Score?

Think of your credit score as your financial report card. Just like your grades in school reflect your academic performance, your credit score reflects your financial behavior. Lenders use a three-digit number, typically ranging from 300 to 850, to assess how likely you are to repay borrowed money. The higher your score, the more financially responsible you appear to potential lenders.

But here's the thing: unlike your school grades, which a single teacher usually determines, your credit score is calculated by complex algorithms using data from your credit reports. And to make things even more interesting, there isn't just one credit score with your name on it.

The two most common types of credit scores are FICO scores and VantageScores. FICO, which stands for Fair Isaac Corporation, is the most widely used. VantageScore, a more recent competitor, was created by the three major credit bureaus: Equifax, Experian, and TransUnion. While both use similar factors to calculate your score, they may weigh these factors differently, resulting in slightly different numbers.

Now, you might wonder, "What's considered a good credit score?" Well, like many things in life, it's relative. Generally speaking, here's how FICO scores break down:

- Excellent: 800-850
- Very Good: 740-799
- Good: 670-739
- Fair: 580-669
- Poor: 300-579

Remember that these ranges can vary slightly depending on the lender and the type of credit you're seeking. For instance, what's considered a good score for a car loan might differ from what's needed for a mortgage.

Let me share a quick story about Alex. When she graduated college, she had no idea what her credit score was or why it mattered. She applied for her first apartment and was shocked when the landlord asked for her credit score. When she checked, her score was in the low 600s - considered "fair" but not great. This experience was a wake-up call for Alex, prompting her to learn more about credit and how to improve her score.

Factors Affecting Your Credit Score

Now that we understand a credit score, let's break down the factors that influence it. Think of your credit score as a cake recipe. Just as different ingredients contribute to the final product in varying amounts, different factors contribute to your credit score in different proportions.

Payment History (35%):

This is the most crucial factor in your credit score calculation.

Payments are the cornerstone of a good credit score. You strengthen your credit profile every time you pay by its due date. Conversely, late payments, missed payments, or accounts sent to collections can significantly damage your score.

Pro tip: Set up automatic payments or reminders to ensure you never miss a due date. Even if you can only make the minimum payment, it's better than missing it entirely.

Credit Utilization (30%):

This refers to how much of your available credit you use at any given time. Keeping your credit utilization low is crucial for maintaining a good credit score. Aim to use no more than 30% of your available credit. For example, if you have a credit card with a $10,000 limit, keep your balance below $3,000. Lower credit utilization signals lenders that you're managing credit responsibly and not overextending yourself financially.

Length of Credit History (15%):

With age comes wisdom - or at least, higher scores in the credit world. The longer you've had credit accounts open and in use, the better. This is why keeping old credit cards open is often advisable, even if you don't use them often.

Credit Mix (10%):

Lenders like to see that you can handle different types of credit responsibly. A mix of revolving credit (like credit cards) and installment loans (like a car loan or mortgage) can positively impact your score.

New Credit (10%):

Opening several new credit accounts in a short period can lower your score. It suggests to lenders that you might be in financial trouble and need access to a lot of credit quickly.

Remember Alex from earlier? After learning about these factors, she realized her low score was largely due to high credit utilization (she was using almost all of her available credit) and a few late payments from when she forgot to pay her credit card bill during finals week. Armed with this knowledge, she planned to improve her score.

Checking Your Credit Score and Report

Now that you know what goes into your credit score, you're probably eager to check your own. Good news: keeping tabs on your credit is easier than ever.

First, let's talk about your credit report. This is the detailed credit history record used to calculate your score. By law, you're entitled to one free credit report from each of the three major credit bureaus yearly. You can access these reports at AnnualCreditReport.com. It's a good idea to spread these out over the year - maybe check one bureau every four months - so you can keep a regular eye on your credit.

But what about your actual credit score? While your free annual credit reports don't include your credit score, there are several ways to check it:

- Many credit card companies now offer free credit score checking as a perk for cardholders.
- Websites like Credit Karma and Credit Sesame provide free credit score estimates.
- You can purchase your FICO score directly from myFICO.com.

Now, you might be wondering about credit monitoring services. These services monitor your credit report and alert you to any changes or potential signs of identity theft. While they can be helpful, especially if you're actively improving your credit or have concerns about identity theft, they're not necessary for everyone. Many of the free services mentioned above offer similar features.

One common concern is whether checking your own credit score will hurt it. The short answer is no. When you check your own score, it's considered a "soft inquiry" and doesn't impact your score. Only when a lender checks your credit as part of a loan application (a "hard inquiry") might there be a small, temporary dip in your score.

Common Credit Score Myths and Misconceptions

Unfortunately, the world of credit scores is rife with myths and misconceptions. Let's just a few of the most common ones:

Myth 1: Checking your credit score lowers it.

As we just discussed, checking your own score is a soft inquiry and doesn't affect your score.

Myth 2: You only have one credit score.

In reality, you have multiple credit scores. Different scoring models (like FICO and VantageScore) may produce different scores, and even within these models, there are variations for different types of loans.

Myth 3: Closing old credit cards will improve your score.

This is often not true. Closing old accounts can actually hurt your score by reducing your overall available credit (increasing your utilization ratio) and potentially shortening your credit history.

Myth 4: You must carry a credit card balance to build credit.

Absolutely not! Paying your balance in full each month is the best way to build credit without paying interest.

Myth 5: Your income affects your credit score.

While income is important for loan applications, it's not a factor in calculating your credit score.

Myth 6: Married couples have a joint credit score.

Each individual has their own credit score, even if they share accounts with a spouse.

Understanding these myths can help you make better decisions about your credit. For instance, I had a colleague who was proud of paying off and closing all her credit cards, thinking it would boost her score. She was surprised when her score dropped due to increased credit utilization and a shortened average account age.

In conclusion, your credit score is crucial to your financial identity. It's a complex calculation based on your credit history, but understanding the basics can help you manage and improve it. Remember, your credit score is not set in stone - it's a dynamic number that can change based on your financial behaviors. You can work towards a healthier credit score by paying bills on time, keeping credit utilization low, maintaining a long credit history, having a mix of credit types, and being cautious about opening new accounts.

As we move forward in this chapter, we'll explore how to use credit cards wisely and build a solid credit history. With the knowledge of how credit scores work, you'll be better equipped to make informed decisions about your credit and overall financial health. Remember, building good credit is a marathon, not a sprint - but with consistent, responsible financial habits, you can achieve a score that opens doors to better financial opportunities.

USING CREDIT CARDS WISELY

Before we dive into the intricacies of using credit cards wisely, let's take a moment to compare credit cards with their close cousin: debit cards. Both plastic rectangles may look similar in your wallet, but they function quite differently and can have vastly different impacts on your financial health.

One of the most significant advantages of credit cards is their ability to help you build a solid credit history. Every on-time payment is like a gold star on your financial report card, potentially boosting your credit score. Credit cards also typically offer stronger fraud protection than debit cards. If someone goes on a shopping spree with your stolen credit card info, you're usually only liable for up to $50, and many cards offer zero liability.

Many credit cards offer rewards for your spending, from cash back to travel miles. Some even throw in perks like travel insurance or extended warranties on purchases. Another advantage is the grace period between your purchase and when you need to pay, giving you some financial flexibility.

However, credit cards aren't without their downsides. If you don't pay your balance in full each month, you'll be hit with interest charges, which can quickly snowball into significant debt. The 'buy now, pay later' nature of credit cards can also lead to overspending if you're not disciplined. Some credit cards, especially rewards cards, charge annual fees that can eat into any benefits you receive.

On the other hand, debit cards draw directly from your bank account, making it harder to overspend. Since you're using your own money, there's no risk of accruing interest. Like credit cards, debit cards are accepted at most merchants and can be used for online purchases.

However, debit cards have their own drawbacks. They offer limited fraud protection compared to credit cards. If someone gets hold of your debit card info, they could drain your bank account. While banks often offer protection, it can take time to get your money back. Using a debit card also doesn't help build your credit history, which can be crucial for future financial opportunities. While some debit cards offer rewards, they're typically not as generous as credit card rewards.

So, which should you use? Like many things in personal finance, the answer depends on your individual situation and financial habits. If you're disciplined with your spending and can pay off your balance in full each month, a credit card can be a powerful tool for building credit and earning rewards. However, a debit card might be the safer choice if you struggle with overspending or are working to get out of debt.

As we move forward in this section, we'll focus on harnessing the power of credit cards while avoiding their potential pitfalls. Remember, credit cards are financial tools – and like any tool, their value depends on how you use them.

Types of Credit Cards

Now that we understand the pros and cons of credit cards versus debit cards, let's dive deeper into the world of credit cards. These little plastic rectangles can be incredibly powerful financial instruments when used correctly, but they can also lead to financial headaches if mismanaged. As we explore the various types of credit cards, remember that choosing the right one is much like selecting the perfect pair of shoes for a specific activity - it's all about finding the best fit for your financial situation and goals.

Credit cards come in many shapes and sizes, each designed to cater to different needs and financial circumstances. Understanding these different types can help you decide which card might be right for you. Let's break down some of the most common types of credit cards you're likely to encounter:

Secured vs. Unsecured Cards:

Secured credit cards are like credit cards with training wheels. They require a cash deposit that typically becomes your credit limit. This deposit acts as collateral, making qualifying cards easier, especially if you have a limited or poor credit history. On the other hand, unsecured cards don't require a deposit but often have stricter approval requirements.

I remember when my younger brother, fresh out of high school, applied for his first credit card. With no credit history, he was denied access to several unsecured cards. He eventually got a secured card with a $500 deposit, which helped him build enough credit to qualify for an unsecured card a year later.

Rewards Cards:

Rewards cards are the overachievers of the credit card world, offering you a little something extra for your everyday spending. These cards typically fall into three main categories, each catering to different lifestyles and preferences:

- **Cash Back Cards:** These are the straightforward crowd-pleasers, giving you a percentage of your purchases back in cold, hard cash. It's like getting a small rebate on everything you buy. For example, a card might offer 2% cash back on all purchases or higher percentages for specific categories like groceries or gas.

- **Travel Points Cards:** The jet setters favorites; these cards help you earn miles or points that can be redeemed for flights, hotel stays, or other travel expenses. They're particularly valuable if you're a frequent traveler or dream of exotic vacations. Some even offer perks like free checked bags or airport lounge access.
- **General Points Cards:** These offer the most flexibility, allowing you to earn points that can be redeemed for various rewards. Whether you're eyeing a new gadget, a gift card to your favorite store, or even a charitable donation, these cards let you choose how to spend your rewards.

The key is to pick a rewards card that aligns with your spending habits and lifestyle to maximize your benefits. Remember, the best rewards are the ones you'll actually use!

Student Credit Cards:

Student credit cards are like the "Credit 101" course of the financial world, designed specifically for college students just starting their credit journey. These cards are the perfect training wheels for building credit responsibility. They often come with lower credit limits, which can be a blessing in disguise, helping students avoid the temptation of over-spending while still allowing them to establish a credit history.

But here's where it gets interesting - many student cards offer perks that speak directly to campus life. Imagine getting cash back for maintaining a good GPA or earning extra points for text-book purchases. It's like getting a financial high-five for your academic efforts!

These cards are typically easier to qualify for than standard credit cards, making them an accessible starting point for students who might not have a long credit history or a steady income. Some even offer educational resources to help students understand credit management better.

However, remember that just because these cards are tailored for students doesn't mean they're one-size-fits-all. It's crucial to compare student cards and choose one that aligns with your needs and spending habits. After all, the goal isn't just to have a credit card but to use it as a tool to build a strong financial foundation for your future.

Benefits of Responsible Credit Card Use

Now that we've explored the different types of credit cards available, let's examine the benefits of responsible credit card use. Credit cards can provide advantages beyond being a convenient payment method when used wisely.

Building a credit history is one of the most significant benefits. Regular use of a credit card, combined with on-time payments, can help establish and improve your credit profile. This is particularly valuable for young adults or anyone looking to strengthen their credit history. Each on-time payment contributes positively to your credit report, gradually building a strong financial reputation.

Many credit cards also offer purchase protection and insurance benefits. These can include extended purchase warranties, protection against theft or damage of recent buys, and even travel insurance. For instance, when I purchased a new laptop last year, my credit card automatically extended the manufacturer's warranty by another year, providing extra peace of mind.

Rewards and perks are another advantage of many credit cards. These can range from cash back on everyday purchases to travel points for frequent flyers. These rewards can provide substantial value when they match your spending habits well. For example, a friend of mine could use the points from her travel rewards card to cover a significant portion of her honeymoon expenses.

Remember, these benefits come from responsible use. The key is using credit cards as a financial tool, not a means to overspend. When used thoughtfully, a credit card can be a helpful instrument in your overall financial strategy.

Strategies for Managing Credit Cards

Now that you know how to use credit cards responsibly, let's dive into the practical details of using them effectively. After all, a credit card is like a financial power tool – incredibly useful when handled correctly but potentially dangerous if misused. So, let's equip ourselves with the knowledge to wield these plastic wonders responsibly.

Paying Balances in Full: The Golden Rule

If there's one credit card commandment to live by, it's this: pay your balance in full each month. It's like returning a library book on time – you get all the benefits without any late fees. Doing this will prevent interest charges and demonstrate responsible credit use. Plus, you'll sleep better at night knowing you're not financially burdened until next month.

Decoding Fees and Interest Rates

Credit cards often have more fine print than a contract for a superhero's secret identity. The most important figure to watch out for is the Annual Percentage Rate (APR) –the yearly interest rate you'll be charged if you carry a balance. But don't stop there. Watch for annual, balance transfer, and foreign transaction fees. Always read the terms and conditions carefully. Yes, it's about as exciting as watching paint dry, but it's crucial to understand what you're signing up for.

The Art of Credit Utilization

Remember our chat about credit utilization in the previous section? It's time to put that knowledge into action. Aim to keep your credit utilization below 30% of your credit limit. Think of it as a financial game of limbo – how low can you go? For instance, if your credit limit is $1,000, try to keep your balance under $300. Your credit score will thank you for it.

The Credit Card Balancing Act: How Many is Too Many?

There's no one-size-fits-all answer regarding the number of credit cards you should have. It's not about collecting cards like Pokémon – quality trumps quantity here. For most people, 2-3 cards hit the sweet spot. This gives you a primary card, a backup for emergencies, and maybe a third to maximize rewards in different spending categories. Any more than that, and you might find yourself juggling more plastic than a circus performer.

By following these strategies, you'll be well on your way to mastering the art of credit card management. Remember, credit cards are financial tools, not magic wands. Use them wisely; they can help build your credit score and even earn you some nice perks along the way. Our next section will explore what to do when the credit card waters get a bit choppy. But for now, pat yourself on the back – you're already ahead of the game in understanding how to use credit cards responsibly.

Avoiding Credit Card Pitfalls

Even the most careful credit card users can stumble without vigilance. Let's explore some common pitfalls to keep an eye out for:

The Minimum Payment Trap:

First up is the minimum payment trap. Paying just the minimum is tempting but can lead to a long-term debt cycle. Here's a sobering example: If you have a $3,000 balance on a card with an 18% APR and only make the minimum payment of $60 monthly, paying off the balance will take over 30 years. Even worse, you'd pay more than $7,000 in interest! That's more than double your original balance.

Balance Transfers: A Double-Edged Sword:

Balance transfers can be useful for consolidating debt and saving on interest, but they're not without risks. Many cards offer 0% interest on balance transfers for a promotional period, which can be a great opportunity to pay down debt. However, be aware of balance transfer fees (typically 3-5% of the transferred amount) and plan for what happens when the promotional period ends.

The Cash Advance Caution:

Using your credit card for a cash advance might seem convenient, but it's often costly. Cash advances usually come with high fees and start accruing interest immediately, with no grace period. It's best to avoid these unless you're in a genuine emergency and have no other options.

By being aware of these potential pitfalls, you're better equipped to use your credit cards wisely. Our next section will discuss what to do if you struggle to make payments. Remember, knowledge is your best defense against credit card mishaps!

What to Do When You Can't Make a Payment

Life has a way of throwing financial curveballs when we least expect them. Even with the best intentions and careful planning, there might be times when you find yourself struggling to make a credit card payment. But don't worry - this doesn't have to be a financial disaster. Let's explore what you can do if you find yourself in this situation.

Communication is Key

First and foremost, don't stick your head in the sand. The worst thing you can do when facing financial difficulties is to ignore the problem. Most credit card companies are more understanding than you might think, especially if you reach out to them proactively. As soon as you realize you might have trouble making a payment, pick up the phone and give them a call.

I can personally attest to the effectiveness of this approach. A few years back, an unexpected medical bill threw my carefully planned budget into chaos. Instead of panicking, I called my credit card company, explained the situation, and was pleasantly surprised by their response. They agreed to push back my due date by two weeks, giving me the breathing room I needed to sort out my finances without incurring a late fee.

Exploring Hardship Programs

Many credit card issuers offer hardship programs designed to help customers navigate temporary financial difficulties. These programs can be a real lifesaver, offering options like reduced interest rates, waived fees, or modified payment plans. However, it's important to understand that these programs often come with certain conditions, such as closing your card or reducing your credit limit.

Some common options you might encounter include:

- Temporarily reduced interest rates
- Waiver of late fees or annual fees
- Permission to skip a payment without penalty
- In more severe cases, the option to work with a credit counseling agency to set up a debt management plan

Remember, these programs are typically reserved for genuine hardships, not just a case of overspending. Be prepared to explain your situation honestly and provide any necessary documentation.

The Long View

As we wrap up our discussion on credit cards, it's important to remember that they're just one piece of your larger financial picture. When used responsibly, credit cards can be powerful tools for building credit, managing cash flow, and even earning rewards. However, they also come with significant responsibilities and potential risks.

In our next section, we'll build on what we've learned about credit scores and credit card management to explore how to build and maintain a good credit history over time. Remember, the goal isn't just to have a high credit score for its own sake. It's about creating a solid financial foundation that opens doors to opportunities and helps you achieve your long-term financial goals. So, let's turn the page and continue our journey towards financial empowerment!

BUILDING A GOOD CREDIT HISTORY

Now that we've explored the fundamentals of credit scores and how they work, let's dive into the art of building a solid credit history. Whether starting from scratch or looking to improve your existing credit profile, this section will equip you with the knowledge and strategies you need to establish a credit history that opens doors to better financial opportunities.

Starting from Scratch: Your First Steps into the World of Credit

For many of us, good credit begins with a blank slate. It's a bit like standing at the edge of an empty canvas, paintbrush in hand, ready to create your financial masterpiece. But where do you start when you have no credit history?

One of the most accessible ways to begin is by becoming an authorized user on someone else's credit card account. Think of it as having a financial mentor willing to lend you their good name – at least in the eyes of credit bureaus. Here's how it works: a family member or trusted friend adds you to their credit card account. You'll get your own card linked to their account, but they remain responsible for the payments. Then, when the account's payment history is reported on your credit report, it helps you build credit by association.

I remember when my younger sister, fresh out of high school, was eager to start building her credit. Our parents added her as an authorized user on their long-standing credit card. Within six months, she had a credit score in the high 600s, giving her a solid foundation upon which to build. However, it's crucial to choose your financial mentor wisely. If they miss payments or maintain high balances, it could negatively impact your budding credit history.

Another powerful tool in your credit-building arsenal is the secured credit card. Think of it as credit with training wheels. You provide a cash deposit that typically becomes your credit limit, acting as collateral. This security blanket makes banks more willing to take a chance on someone with no credit history. The key is to use the card responsibly – make small, regular purchases and pay the balance in full each month. Keep your credit utilization below 30% of your limit, and you'll be on your way to establishing a positive credit history.

I once worked with a client, Alex, who was frustrated by his lack of credit history. We started him off with a secured card with a $500 limit. He used it to pay for his monthly phone bill and groceries, always paying the balance in full. After just eight months of responsible use, he was offered an unsecured card with a higher limit and even some rewards. It was a small step that opened up a world of financial opportunities for him.

As you embark on your credit-building journey, remember that consistency is key. Whether an authorized user or using a secured card, make every payment on time. Set up automatic payments if needed – your future self will thank you. And don't be discouraged if you don't see results overnight. Building credit is a marathon, not a sprint.

Advancing Your Credit Game: Strategies for Growth

Once you've established a baseline credit history, leveling up your credit game is time. This is where we move from finger painting to creating financial masterpieces. Let's explore some advanced strategies to maintain and improve your credit.

First, let's talk about optimizing your credit mix. Remember how we discussed that credit mix accounts for 10% of your credit score? Now's the time to put that knowledge into action. Aim for a diverse credit portfolio – a mix of revolving credit (like credit cards) and installment loans (like a car or personal loans). This diversity shows lenders that you can handle various types of credit responsibly.

As your credit improves, it's time to prioritize your credit utilization. While we've emphasized keeping your utilization below 30%, aim for the sweet spot between 1-10% for optimal credit scores. One clever trick is to time your payments. Pay down your credit card balances just before the statement closing date to report lower utilization to credit bureaus. It's like showing up to a job interview in your best suit – you want to present the best possible picture of your financial habits.

Don't be afraid to request credit limit increases on your existing cards. This can lower your overall utilization if you don't increase your spending. Be strategic about when you ask – time these requests when your income increases or after a period of excellent payment history. It's like asking for a raise at work – you want to do it when you've proven your value.

Transitioning to Advanced Credit Management

As you move from basic credit-building to more sophisticated credit management, it's time to graduate from your secured credit card to unsecured cards. After 12-18 months of responsible secured card use, you'll likely qualify for an unsecured card. Look for cards with rewards programs that match your spending habits. But here's a pro tip: consider keeping your secured card open. It contributes to your length of credit history and your total available credit, which can positively impact your score.

Timing is everything, especially when it comes to applying for new credit. Space out your credit applications to minimize the impact of hard inquiries on your score. And be strategic about when you apply. If you know you'll need to finance a major purchase shortly, avoid applying for new credit in the months leading up to it. You want your score to be in top shape when needed.

Lastly, don't forget about your older accounts. In the world of credit, age is beauty. Keep your oldest credit accounts open and active, even if you don't use them often. Set up a small recurring charge and automatic payment to keep them active without effort. It's like tending to a garden – a little regular care goes a long way in maintaining a healthy credit ecosystem.

The Long Game: Sustaining Good Credit

Building a good credit history is not a "set it and forget it" endeavor. It requires ongoing attention and care. Think of it as a lifelong financial fitness regimen. Just as you wouldn't expect to get in shape by going to the gym once and never again, you can't expect to maintain good credit without consistent effort.

Make it a habit to review your credit reports regularly. You're entitled to one free credit report from each major credit bureau annually. Spread these out – check one bureau every four months. This regular check-up lets you spot any errors or potential signs of identity theft early.

Speaking of identity theft, you become a more attractive target for fraudsters as your credit improves. Be vigilant about protecting your personal information. Use strong, unique passwords for all your financial accounts, and consider placing a security freeze on your credit reports. It's like putting a lock on your financial front door – an extra layer of protection against potential threats.

Remember, building and maintaining good credit takes time. Your credit needs will evolve as your life circumstances change. Getting married, buying a home, or starting a business – all these life events can impact your credit. Stay informed, be proactive, and don't be afraid to seek professional advice when needed.

In conclusion, building a good credit history is one of the most powerful steps toward financial freedom. It opens doors to better loan terms, lower insurance rates, and even job opportunities. But more than that, it gives you the peace of mind that comes with knowing you're in control of your financial destiny.

Congratulations! You've now built a solid financial knowledge foundation, from understanding your money mindset to mastering budgeting and credit management. It's time to put this knowledge into action. In the next chapter, we'll embark on a 5-week action plan that combines everything you've learned. You'll apply your budgeting skills, implement saving strategies, manage credit wisely, and work towards your financial goals. Get ready to transform your financial life, one week at a time!

CHAPTER 5
YOUR ACTION PLAN FOR MONEY SUCCESS

Congratulations! By now, you've gained a wealth of knowledge about personal finance, from understanding your money mindset to mastering the art of budgeting and credit management. But knowledge alone isn't enough to transform your financial life. It's time to turn that knowledge into action.

This chapter is all about creating your personalized action plan for financial success. Think of it as your roadmap to financial freedom. We'll mold everything you've learned so far into a concrete plan that fits your unique situation and goals. Whether you're just starting your career, trying to pay off debt, or looking to build wealth for the future, this chapter will help you chart your course.

You wouldn't set out on a cross-country road trip without a map (or at least a GPS), would you? Similarly, navigating your financial future without a plan is like reaching a destination without directions. Your personal financial plan is that map – it shows you where you are, where you want to go, and how to get there.

Creating this plan isn't just about crunching numbers or setting arbitrary goals. It's about aligning your finances with your values and dreams. It's about taking control of your money so that it works for you rather than vice versa.

I remember when I first started my financial journey. I had a vague idea that I wanted to be "financially stable," but I had no concrete plan. I was like a ship without a rudder, drifting wherever the financial winds took me. It wasn't until I sat down and created a detailed action plan that I saw real progress. That plan became my financial North Star, guiding my decisions and keeping me on track even when life threw curveballs my way.

Your action plan will be unique to you. It will reflect your goals, current situation, and the financial strategies that resonate with you. But don't worry – we'll go through this process step by step, building on everything you've learned in the previous chapters.

WEEK 1 - LAYING THE FOUNDATION

Alright, let's dive into Week 1 of your financial transformation journey. This week is all about laying a solid foundation for your financial future. Remember, just as a house needs a strong foundation to withstand the test of time, your financial life needs a sturdy base to weather life's ups and downs. So, let's roll up our sleeves and get started!

Action Steps for Week 1:

1. Gather all financial documents and calculate your net worth and monthly cash flow.
2. Track every expense for seven days straight.
3. Spend 30 minutes reflecting on your money mindset and write down any limiting beliefs you identify.

4. Set three SMART financial goals and post them where you'll see them daily.

1. Assessing Your Current Financial Situation

The first step in any journey is knowing where you're starting from. This week, we will take a clear-eyed look at your current financial picture. Don't worry if it's not pretty – the point isn't to judge but to understand.

Start by gathering all your financial documents: bank statements, credit card bills, loan statements, pay stubs, and any investment account information. Now, let's crunch some numbers:

Calculate your net worth: List all your assets (what you own) and subtract your liabilities (what you owe). This gives you a snapshot of your financial health.

Determine your monthly income: Include your salary and other regular income sources.

List all your regular monthly expenses: Don't forget annual expenses – divide them by 12 to get a monthly figure.

This process might feel overwhelming, but remember, knowledge is power. Understanding where you stand financially is the first step towards improvement.

2. Tracking Expenses for a Full Week

Now that you have a bird's eye view of your finances, it's time to zoom in. For the next seven days, I want you to track every single expense. Yes, even that $2 coffee or that $1 vending machine snack. Use a notebook, spreadsheet, or budgeting app – whatever works for you.

This exercise isn't about restriction; it's about awareness. You might be surprised where your money is actually going. Are those small daily purchases adding up more than you realized? Is there a category where you're spending more than you thought? This week-long snapshot will give you valuable insights into your spending habits.

3. Identifying Your Money Mindset and Potential Limiting Beliefs

As discussed in Chapter 1, your money mindset is crucial to your financial life. This week, take some time to reflect on your attitudes and beliefs about money. Ask yourself:

- What did I learn about money growing up?
- Do I believe money is scarce or abundant?
- Do I feel confident managing money, or does it make me anxious?
- What's my biggest fear when it comes to money?

Be honest with yourself. Identifying any limiting beliefs is the first step to overcoming them. Remember, your beliefs shape your actions, shaping your financial reality.

4. Setting SMART Financial Goals

Now that you clearly understand where you stand and what might hold you back, it's time to look forward. This week, set at least three SMART financial goals – one short-term (within the next year), one medium-term (1-5 years), and one long-term (5+ years).

Remember, SMART goals are the cornerstone of effective financial planning. They should be Specific, clearly defining what you want to achieve; Measurable, allowing you to quantify your progress; Achievable, realistic given your current situation; Relevant, aligning with your values and long-term objectives; and Time-bound, having a specific timeframe for completion.

For example, instead of "save more money," a SMART goal would be "Save $2,000 for an emergency fund by December 31st of this year by setting aside $180 per month."

Write these goals down and put them somewhere visible. They'll be your financial North Star in the coming weeks and months.

Action Steps for Week 1 Review:

- Gather all financial documents and calculate your net worth and monthly cash flow.
- Track every expense for seven days straight.
- Spend 30 minutes reflecting on your money mindset and write down any limiting beliefs you identify.
- Set three SMART financial goals and post them where you'll see them daily.

Remember, this week is about building awareness and setting intentions. Don't judge yourself for what you discover – simply observe and learn. Every financial journey starts with a single step, and you've just taken a big one. Be proud of yourself for taking control of your financial future!

Next week, we'll use the insights you've gained to create a budget that aligns with your goals and values. But for now, focus on completing this week's tasks. You're laying the foundation for a brighter financial future, and that's something to celebrate!

WEEK 2 - BUDGETING BOOTCAMP AND EMERGENCY FUND

Excellent work on tracking your expenses and setting your financial goals last week! Now that you have a clearer picture of your spending habits, it's time to create a budget that aligns with your financial objectives. This week, we'll focus on crafting your budget, cutting unnecessary expenses, and kickstarting your emergency fund. Let's dive into Week 2 - Budgeting Bootcamp and Emergency Fund Initiation!

Action Steps for Week 2:

1. Create your first budget based on last week's expense tracking.
2. Choose and implement a budgeting method that works for you.
3. Identify and cut at least three unnecessary expenses.
4. Start an emergency fund or increase your current contributions.

1. Creating Your First Budget Based on the Previous Week's Tracking

Remember all those expenses you meticulously tracked last week? It's time to put that data to work. Start by categorizing your expenses - housing, transportation, food, entertainment, etc. Then, compare these actual expenses to your income. This comparison will give you a realistic picture of where your money is going and where you might need adjustments.

Now, create a budget that reflects your actual spending and financial goals. Be honest with yourself, but also be ambitious. Your budget should challenge you to do better while remaining achievable. Remember, a budget isn't about restriction - it's about intentionality. It's deciding in advance where you want your money to go rather than wondering where it went.

2. Implementing a Chosen Budgeting Method

There are various budgeting methods; the best one is the one you'll stick to. Let's revisit two popular methods we discussed in Chapter 3:

The 50/30/20 Method suggests allocating 50% of your income to needs, 30% to wants, and 20% to savings and debt repayment. It's simple and flexible, making it great for budgeting beginners.

Zero-Based Budgeting: You assign every dollar to a job using this method. Your income minus your expenses (including savings) should equal zero. It's more time-intensive but gives you maximum control over your money.

Choose the method that resonates with you and align it with the financial goals you set last week. Remember, your budget is a living document. You'll refine it over time as you learn more about your spending habits and your financial situation evolves.

3. Identify and cut at least three unnecessary expenses

Now, many people dread cutting expenses. But remember, this isn't about deprivation. It's about aligning your spending with your values and goals. Look at your categorized expenses and ask yourself:

- Does this expense align with my values and goals?
- Is there a way to reduce this expense without significantly impacting my quality of life?

- Am I getting good value for this expense, or could I find a better deal?
- Be creative in finding ways to cut costs. Could you negotiate a better rate on your cell phone plan? What about carpooling to work to save on gas? Could you cut back on dining out and discover the joy of cooking at home instead?

Here's a challenge: try to find at least three expenses you can reduce or eliminate this week. Put the money you save towards your financial goals. You might be surprised at how empowering it feels to redirect your money this way.

4. Starting or Increasing Contributions to an Emergency Fund

An emergency fund is your financial safety net, protecting you from unexpected expenses or income loss. If you don't have an emergency fund, now's the time to start. If you do, consider increasing your contributions.

Aim to eventually save 3-6 months of living expenses in your emergency fund. This might seem daunting, but remember – you'll do this for the long haul. Start with a smaller goal, like $1,000, then work your way up.

Here's a step-by-step approach:

1. Determine your monthly essential expenses.
2. Set a target amount (start with $1,000, then aim for 3-6 times your monthly expenses).
3. Decide how much you can contribute each month. Even small amounts add up over time!
4. Open a separate savings account specifically for your emergency fund.

5. Set up automatic transfers to your emergency fund account.

Keep your emergency fund in an easily accessible savings account. You want this money to be there when you need it, but it is not so accessible that you're tempted to dip into it for non-emergencies.

Review Action Steps for Week 2:

- Create your first budget based on last week's expense tracking.
- Choose and implement a budgeting method that works for you.
- Identify and cut at least three unnecessary expenses.
- Start an emergency fund or increase your current contributions.

As you work through these steps, remember that budgeting and saving are skills that improve with practice. Don't be discouraged if you don't get it perfect right away. This week's goal is to create a realistic budget, cut unnecessary expenses, and build your financial safety net.

Pay attention to how it feels to spend according to your budget. Does it feel restrictive or give you a sense of control? Are there areas where you need to allocate more money or places where you could cut back further? Keep notes on these observations - they'll be valuable as you refine your budget in the coming weeks.

You're making fantastic progress in taking control of your financial life. By creating a budget, cutting unnecessary expenses, and starting an emergency fund, you're setting yourself up for long-term financial success. Keep up the great work!

Next week, we'll focus on managing credit and tackling debt. But for now, concentrate on implementing your new budget and making those first contributions to your emergency fund. Remember, no matter how small, every step you take moves you closer to your financial goals. You've got this!

WEEK 3 - CREDIT CHECK AND DEBT TACKLING

Fantastic progress on creating and implementing your budget! As we enter Week 3, we'll shift our focus to an aspect of personal finance that can significantly impact your financial health: credit. Understanding and managing your credit is crucial for achieving long-term financial success. So, let's roll up our sleeves and dive into the world of credit reports, debt repayment, and responsible credit use.

Action Steps for Week 3:

1. Obtain and review your credit reports from all three bureaus.
2. Create a debt repayment plan if applicable.
3. Implement at least three strategies to improve your credit score.
4. Review your credit card usage and plan for responsible use.

1. Obtaining and Reviewing Your Credit Report

Your credit report is like a financial report card that lenders use to assess your creditworthiness. This week, your first task is to obtain a free copy of your credit report from each of the three major credit bureaus: Equifax, Experian, and TransUnion. You can do this at AnnualCreditReport.com.

Once you have your reports, could you review them carefully? Look for errors or discrepancies, such as accounts you don't recognize or incorrect personal information. If you find any errors, dispute them immediately with the credit bureau. Even small errors can impact your credit score, so this step is crucial.

Pay close attention to the following sections:

- Personal Information: Ensure all details are correct.
- Credit Accounts: Verify all accounts listed belong to you and the information is accurate.
- Public Records: Look for any negative items like bankruptcies or liens.

Remember, knowledge is power. Understanding what's in your credit report is the first step to taking control of your credit.

2. Creating a Debt Repayment Plan

If you have debt, now's the time to create a strategic plan to pay it off. Start by listing all your debts, including the creditor, balance, interest rate, and minimum payment for each. This gives you a clear picture of what you're dealing with.

Next, choose a debt repayment strategy. Two popular methods are:

- The Debt Avalanche: Focus on paying off the debt with the highest interest rate first while making minimum payments on others. This method saves you the most money in interest over time.
- The Debt Snowball: Pay off the smallest debt first, then roll that payment into the next smallest debt. This method provides quick wins and can be more motivating.

Choose the method that aligns best with your financial situation and personality. Remember, the best strategy is the one you'll stick to consistently.

Allocate any extra money in your budget towards your chosen debt repayment strategy. Even small additional payments can significantly reduce the time it takes to become debt-free.

3. Implementing Strategies to Improve Your Credit Score

Now that you understand your credit report and have a debt repayment plan, let's focus on improving your credit score. Here are some key strategies:

- **Payment History (35% of your FICO score):** Always pay your bills promptly. Set up automatic payments or reminders to ensure you never miss a due date.
- **Credit Utilization (30% of your score):** Keep your credit card balances low. Aim to use no more than 30% of your available credit.
- **Length of Credit History (15% of your score):** Keep old accounts open, even if you don't use them often. A long credit history can positively impact your score.
- **Credit Mix (10% of your score):** A mix of credit types (credit cards, installment loans) can improve your score. However, don't open new accounts just for this reason.
- **New Credit (10% of your score):** Limit how often you apply for new credit. Each application can result in a hard inquiry, temporarily lowering your score.

Remember, improving your credit score takes time. Be patient and consistent in your efforts.

4. Learning to Use Credit Cards Responsibly

Credit cards can be powerful financial tools when used wisely. Here are some tips for responsible credit card use:

- Pay your balance in full each month to avoid interest charges.
- If you can't pay in full, always pay more than the minimum.
- Use your card for planned purchases, not impulsive spending.
- Take advantage of rewards programs, but don't let them tempt you into overspending.
- Regularly review your statements for errors or fraudulent charges.

Consider setting up balance alerts to notify you when your balance reaches a certain threshold. This can help you stay mindful of your spending and avoid overuse.

Review Action Steps for Week 3:

1. Obtain and review your credit reports from all three bureaus.
2. Create a debt repayment plan if applicable.
3. Implement at least three strategies to improve your credit score.
4. Review your credit card usage and plan for responsible use.

As you work through this week's tasks, remember that managing credit and debt is ongoing. It requires consistent effort and mindful decision-making. But the payoff is worth it – a strong credit profile can open doors to better financial opportunities and save you money in the long run.

You're making great strides in taking control of your financial life. By understanding your credit, tackling debt, and using credit responsibly, you're setting yourself up for long-term financial success. Keep up the fantastic work!

Next week, we'll focus on supercharging your savings and building a robust emergency fund. But for now, concentrate on implementing these credit and debt strategies. You're not just managing your money but building a solid financial foundation for your future. Keep pushing forward – you've got this!

WEEK 4 - SAVING AND EMERGENCY FUND BUILDING

Great progress on managing your credit and tackling debt! Now that you've got a handle on your day-to-day finances and credit situation, it's time to look further into the future. Welcome to Week 4, where we'll focus on setting long-term financial goals and supercharging your savings. Remember, building wealth is not just about managing your current finances—it's about planning for the future and making your money work harder. Let's dive in!

Action Steps for Week 4:

1. Set at least three long-term financial goals.
2. Implement two new strategies to boost your savings rate.
3. Research a high-yield savings option for at least one of your savings goals.

1. Setting Long-Term Financial Goals

Long-term financial planning is about identifying what you want your financial life to look like in 5, 10, or even 20 years from now. It's about dreaming big and creating a roadmap to realize those dreams.

Start by asking yourself some big questions:

- What does financial success look like to me?
- Where do I want to be financially in 5 years? 10 years? At retirement?
- What major life events do I anticipate (buying a home, starting a family, changing careers)?

Use your answers to set SMART long-term financial goals. Remember, SMART goals are Specific, Measurable, Achievable, Relevant, and Time-bound. Here are some examples:

- "Save $50,000 for a house down payment in 5 years."
- "Increase my retirement contributions to 15% of my income within 3 years."
- "Pay off all non-mortgage debt within 7 years."

Aim to set at least three long-term financial goals. Write these goals down and place them somewhere visible. They'll serve as your financial North Star, guiding your decisions and motivating you.

2. Implementing Strategies to Boost Your Savings Rate

Now that you have your long-term goals in sight, it's time to turbocharge your savings to help you get there faster. Here are some strategies to boost your savings rate:

- The 52-Week Money Challenge: Save $1 in week one, $2 in week two, and so on. By the end of the year, you'll have saved $1,378.
- The 1% Increase: Boost your monthly savings rate by 1%. If you're saving 5% of your income now, aim for 6% next month, 7% the month after, and so on.
- Save Your Raises and Bonuses: Whenever you get a pay increase or bonus, immediately divert that extra money to savings before spending it.
- Use Cashback Apps and Credit Cards: Put the cashback you earn directly into savings.
- Try a No-Spend Challenge: Choose a week (or even a month) where you only spend on absolute essentials. Put all the money you save into your savings account.
- Automate Your Savings: Set up automatic transfers to your savings account on payday. What you don't see, you won't miss.

Choose at least two of these strategies to implement this week. Remember, the key to successful saving is consistency. Even small increases in your savings rate can lead to significant results over time, thanks to the power of compound interest.

3. Researching and Choosing High-Yield Savings Options

Now that you're boosting your savings rate, let's make sure your money is working as hard as possible for you. High-yield savings options offer better interest rates than traditional savings accounts, allowing your money to grow faster.

Here are some options to consider:

- **High-Yield Savings Accounts:** Many online banks

offer these accounts with interest rates significantly higher than traditional banks.

- **Money Market Accounts:** These often offer higher rates than traditional savings accounts and may include check-writing privileges.
- **Certificates of Deposit (CDs):** These offer higher rates in exchange for leaving your money untouched for a set period.
- **I Bonds:** These government savings bonds are tied to inflation and can offer attractive rates, especially in high-inflation environments.
- **Cash Management Accounts:** Offered by some investment firms, these can provide high interest rates and other features like checking and investment options.

When researching these options, consider factors like:

- Interest rates
- Minimum balance requirements
- Fees
- Accessibility of funds
- FDIC insurance

Choose at least one of your savings goals and research the best high-yield option. For example, a high-yield savings account or a CD ladder might be appropriate if you save for a house down payment in five years. Consider I Bonds or a cash management account if saving for a longer-term goal.

Review Action Steps for Week 4:

- Set at least three long-term financial goals.
- Implement two new strategies to boost your savings rate.

- Research and choose a high-yield savings option for at least one of your savings goals.

As you work through these steps, remember that long-term financial planning is about balancing your current needs with your future aspirations. It might feel challenging to save more now, but your future self will thank you for the financial security and opportunities you're creating.

You're doing an incredible job taking control of your finances! By setting long-term goals, boosting your savings, and exploring high-yield options, you're not just managing your money but actively growing your wealth.

Next week, we'll wrap up our 5-week plan by reviewing your progress, setting up systems for your various savings goals, and creating a plan for continuous financial improvement. But for now, focus on those long-term goals and supercharging your savings. Remember, every extra dollar you save is a step towards your dream future. Keep up the fantastic work—you're building a financial foundation that will serve you well for years!

WEEK 5 - REFINING YOUR FINANCIAL SYSTEM

Congratulations on reaching the final week of our action plan! You've made incredible progress over the past month, tackling everything from budgeting to long-term goal setting. It's time to fine-tune your financial system and set yourself up for ongoing success. This week, we'll focus on reviewing your progress, setting up a robust savings structure, and creating a plan for continuous financial growth. Let's dive into Week 5 - Refining Your Financial System!

Action Steps for Week 5:

1. Review and adjust your budget based on the past month's spending.
2. Set up separate savings accounts for at least three financial goals.
3. Set up automated transfers to your savings accounts.
4. Create a plan for ongoing financial education, committing to at least one monthly learning activity.

1. Reviewing and Adjusting Your Budget Based on the Past Month's Spending

You've been working with your budget for a month now, and it's time for a thorough review. How well did your budget align with your actual spending? Where did you succeed, and where did you struggle?

Start by comparing your planned budget with your actual spending over the past month. Look for patterns:

- **Overspending:** Which categories consistently went over budget?
- **Underspending:** Where did you spend less than expected?
- **Forgotten Expenses:** Did any unexpected costs pop up?

Use these insights to adjust your budget. Maybe you underestimated your grocery costs or overestimated your entertainment spending. That's okay! Budgeting is an iterative process that takes time to get it right.

Remember, a good budget should feel a little uncomfortable, but possible. If you're consistently overspending in a category, consider whether you need to allocate more money there or find ways to cut back. The goal is to create a realistic budget aligned with your financial goals.

2. Setting Up Separate Savings Accounts for Different Goals

Now that you have a handle on your spending and have set long-term financial goals, it's time to create a savings structure that supports these goals. One of the most effective ways to manage your savings is to create separate accounts for different financial objectives. This method, often called "bucketing" or "envelope budgeting," helps you visualize your progress toward each goal and reduces the temptation to dip into savings meant for other purposes.

Review your long-term financial goals from last week and identify at least three that require dedicated savings. These might include:

- Emergency Fund
- Retirement Savings (beyond your 401(k) or IRA)
- House Down Payment
- Dream Vacation
- New Car Fund

Open separate savings accounts for each of these goals. Online banks allow you to create multiple savings accounts with no additional fees. Name each account according to its purpose: to keep yourself motivated and focused.

3. Setting Up Automated Transfers to Your Savings Accounts

Now that your savings buckets are set up, it's time to ensure they're consistently filled. Automation is your best friend when it comes to saving money. By setting up automatic transfers, you're paying your future self-first before you have a chance to spend the money elsewhere.

Here's how to set up your automated savings system:

1. Determine how much you can save towards each goal based on your budget.
2. Decide on the frequency of transfers (weekly, bi-weekly, or monthly).
3. Set up automatic transfers from your checking account to each savings account.
4. Schedule these transfers to occur right after your payday.

Start with whatever amount you can, even if it's small. You can always increase the amount as your financial situation improves. The key is to make saving a habit, and automation helps ensure that habit sticks.

4. Creating a Plan for Ongoing Financial Education

Financial literacy is a lifelong journey. Markets change, new financial products emerge, and your personal circumstances evolve. It would be best to have an ongoing learning and improvement plan to stay on top of your finances.

Here are some strategies to continue your financial education:

- **Read Financial Books:** Commit to reading one personal finance book every quarter.
- **Follow Financial Blogs and Podcasts:** Choose 2-3 reputable sources and follow them regularly.
- **Attend Workshops or Webinars:** Many banks, credit

unions, and community organizations offer free financial education sessions.
- **Use Financial Management Tools:** Explore apps and software that can help you track your progress and provide financial insights.
- **Take Online Courses:** Platforms like Coursera and edX offer free financial courses from top universities.
- **Join a Financial Book Club or Discussion Group:** Sharing ideas with others can deepen your understanding and provide new perspectives.

Commit to at least one learning activity per month. Schedule it in your calendar like any other important appointment. Remember, investing in your financial education is one of the best investments you can make.

Review Action Steps for Week 5:

1. Review and adjust your budget based on the past month's spending.
2. Set up separate savings accounts for at least three financial goals.
3. Set up automated transfers to your savings accounts.
4. Create a plan for ongoing financial education, committing to at least one monthly learning activity.

As we wrap up our 5-week action plan, take a moment to reflect on how far you've come. You've laid a solid foundation for your financial future, from understanding your money mindset to creating a budget, setting long-term goals, and refining your financial system.

Remember, financial success is not about perfection—it's about progress. There will be setbacks along the way, but with the tools and knowledge you've gained, you're well-equipped to handle whatever financial challenges come your way.

Keep revisiting the strategies we've discussed, stay committed to your goals, and never stop learning. Your financial journey is just beginning, and the future is bright. By consistently applying what you've learned and continuing to educate yourself, you're setting yourself up for long-term financial success.

Congratulations on completing this 5-week financial transformation! You've taken significant steps towards mastering your money. Keep up the great work, stay curious, and remember—every financial decision you make is a step toward the future you envision. Here's to your continued financial success!

CHAPTER 6
YOUR FINANCIAL FUTURE STARTS NOW

Congratulations! You've reached the final chapter of "Master Your Money: A Practical Guide to Financial Freedom." But remember, this isn't the end—it's just the beginning of your journey towards financial mastery. Throughout this book, we've explored the essential components of a solid financial foundation, from understanding your money mindset to creating a budget, managing debt, building savings, and planning for the future.

As you embark on your personal finance journey, it's important to recognize that challenges will inevitably arise. You might face unexpected expenses, experience income fluctuations, or feel overwhelmed by the complexities of investing. These obstacles are a normal part of the financial journey, and they're not signs of failure—they're growth opportunities.

I remember when I first started taking control of my finances. I was excited about my new budget and determined to stick to it religiously. But just two weeks in, my car broke down, requiring an expensive repair I hadn't accounted for. At first, I felt defeated. Had I failed already? But then I realized this was exactly why I was working on my finances. I dipped into my fledgling emergency fund, adjusted my budget for the next few months, and learned the importance of building more flexibility into my financial plan.

This experience taught me a valuable lesson: financial setbacks are not failures; they're learning opportunities. Each challenge you face will make you more resilient and financially savvy. So, don't get discouraged when encountering obstacles—and you will. Instead, view them as chances to refine your strategies and strengthen your financial foundation.

Sound financial management's long-term benefits extend beyond having more money in your bank account. When you take control of your finances, you're investing in your future self. You're creating a life of reduced stress, increased freedom, and expanded opportunities.

Imagine waking up each day knowing you have a robust emergency fund to handle life's unexpected turns. Picture the peace of mind that comes from having a clear path out of debt and investments steadily growing for your future. Envision the joy of saying "yes" to experiences and opportunities that truly matter to you without financial stress holding you back.

This financial peace of mind ripples through all aspects of your life. It lets you focus more on your passions, relationships, and personal growth. It allows you to make career decisions based on fulfillment rather than just paycheck size. It enables you to be more generous, supporting causes you care about and helping others. In essence, sound financial management doesn't just secure your financial future—it enhances your overall quality of life.

As you continue your financial journey, remember that learning never stops. The world of personal finance is constantly evolving, with new tools, strategies, and challenges always emerging. To stay informed and continue building your financial knowledge, I encourage you to visit www.path2better.com. This website is packed with up-to-date information, practical resources, and expert insights to support you on your path to financial freedom.

Speaking of evolving, let's touch on some emerging trends in personal finance that you should keep an eye on:

- **Cryptocurrency and Blockchain:** While volatile, these technologies are increasingly becoming part of the financial landscape. Educate yourself about their potential benefits and risks.
- **Sustainable Investing:** More investors want to align their portfolios with their values, leading to a rise in ESG (Environmental, Social, and Governance) investing options.
- **Fintech Innovation:** From robo-advisors to peer-to-peer lending platforms, technology is making financial services more accessible and personalized than ever before.
- **The Gig Economy:** With more people engaging in freelance and contract work, financial strategies must adapt to less predictable income streams.
- **Artificial Intelligence in Personal Finance:** AI-powered tools are becoming more sophisticated in helping individuals budget, invest, and plan for the future.

While these trends offer exciting opportunities, they also underscore the importance of ongoing financial education. Stay curious, keep learning, and don't be afraid to adapt your strategies as the financial world evolves.

As we conclude this book, I want to leave you with this message: Your financial future is yours. Every decision you make, from the small daily choices to the big life-changing moves, shapes your financial reality. You have the power to create the financial life you desire.

Remember, financial freedom isn't about having unlimited wealth—it's about having enough. Enough to live comfortably, pursue your passions, help others, and face the future confidently. And "enough" is different for everyone. Your financial journey is uniquely yours, shaped by your values, goals, and circumstances.

So, I challenge you: take that first step today. Whether tracking your expenses, setting up a savings account, or simply committing to read about finance for 15 minutes each day, do something that moves you closer to your financial goals. Remember, every journey begins with a single step, and you've already taken several by reading this book.

There will be times when you feel overwhelmed or unsure. In those moments, return to the basics we've covered in this book. Revisit your budget, review your goals, and remember why you started this journey. And don't hesitate to seek help—whether from the resources at **www.path2better.com**, financial professionals, or supportive friends and family.

You've got this. You have the knowledge, tools, and motivation to take control of your financial life. Your journey to financial freedom starts now, and it will be an exciting ride. There will be challenges but also victories, learning experiences, and the immense satisfaction of watching your financial health improve over time.

So go forth with confidence. Make those smart financial decisions. Celebrate your progress, learn from your setbacks, and keep moving forward. Your future self will thank you for the financial security and freedom you're creating today.

Here's to your journey towards financial freedom—may it be rewarding, enlightening, and ultimately, life-changing. You have the power to master your money and create the life you envision. Now, it's time to turn that vision into reality. Your financial transformation begins now!

YOUR OPINION MATTERS!

Dear Reader,

As you've reached this point in "Broke no More: The Gen Z Guide to Money Mastery in 5 Weeks," I hope you've gained valuable insights and practical strategies to transform your financial life.

Why Your Review is Important

Your feedback is invaluable. It helps:

- Other young adults decide if this book is right for their financial journey
- I understand how to improve and create even better resources for Gen Z's financial education
- Boost the visibility of this book, allowing it to reach more people who could benefit from these money mastery strategies.

Ready to Share Your Thoughts? It takes just a few minutes to make a big impact. Leave Your Review Here

LOOKING FOR MORE PERSONAL FINANCE RESOURCES?

Visit my website for free tools, guides, and resources that will help you continue mastering your finances and achieving your dreams.

💡 **Explore investment tips, budgeting, debt management strategies, and more.**
🔗 **Check it out here: www.Path2Better.com**

Made in the USA
Monee, IL
04 November 2026

67386703R00079